The Pocket

FISHING
BASICS
GUIDE

Freshwater Basics: Hook, Line & Sinker

by Wade Bourne

StoegerBooks

STOEGER PUBLISHING COMPANY
is a division of Benelli U.S.A.

Benelli U.S.A.
Vice President and General Manager:
Stephen Otway
Vice President of Marketing and Communications:
Stephen McKelvain

Stoeger Publishing Company
President: Jeffrey Reh
Publisher: Jennifer Thomas
Managing Editor: Harris J. Andrews
Creative Director: Cynthia T. Richardson
Graphic Designer: William Graves
Special Accounts Manager: Julie Brownlee
Publishing Assistant: Stacy Logue

Illustration: William Graves
Proofreader: Stacy Logue

Published by:
Stoeger Publishing Company
17603 Indian Head Highway, Suite 200
Accokeek, Maryland 20607

BK0703
ISBN-13: 978-0-88317-345-9
ISBN-10: 0-88317-345-X
Library of Congress Control Number:
LC 2007923411

Manufactured in the United States of America.

*Distributed to the book trade and
to the sporting goods trade by:*
Stoeger Industries
17603 Indian Head Highway, Suite 200
Accokeek, Maryland 20607
301 283-6300   Fax: 301 283-6986
www.stoegerpublishing.com

OTHER PUBLICATIONS:

Shooter's Bible
The World's Standard
Firearms Reference Book
Gun Trader's Guide
Complete Fully Illustrated
Guide to Modern Firearms
with Current Market Values

Hunting & Shooting:
Beretta Pistols
The Bowhunter's Guide
The Pocket Deer
Hunting Guide
Elk Hunter's Bible
High Performance Muzzleloading
Big Game Rifles
High Power Rifle Accuracy:
Before You Shoot
Hunt Club Management Guide
Hunting Tough Bucks
Hunting Whitetails East & West
Hunting the Whitetail Rut
Modern Shotgunning
Shotgunning for Deer
Taxidermy Guide
Tennessee Whitetails
Trailing the Hunter's Moon
The Turkey Hunter's Tool Kit:
Shooting Savvy
The Ultimate in Rifle Accuracy
Whitetail Strategies

Firearms:
Antique Guns:
A Collector's Guide
Guns & Ammo:
The Shooter's Guide to
Clasic Firearms
Gunsmithing Made Easy
How to Buy & Sell Used Guns
Model 1911: Automatic Pistol
Modern Beretta Firearms

Reloading:
The Handloader's Manual of
Cartridge Conversions 3rd Ed.

Fishing:
Big Bass Zone
Catfishing: Beyond the Basics
The Crappie Book
Fishing Made Easy
Fishing Online:
1,000 Best Web Sites
Flyfishing for Trout A-Z
Out There Fishing
Practical Bowfishing
The Walleye Pro's Notebook

Cooking Game:
The Complete Book of
Dutch Oven Cooking
Dress 'Em Out
Wild About Freshwater Fish
Wild About Game Birds
Wild About Seafood
Wild About Venison
Wild About Waterfowl
World's Best Catfish Cookbook

Nature:
The Pocket Disaster
Survival Guide
The Pocket First-Aid
Field Guide
The Pocket Outdoor
Survival Guide
U.S. Guide to Venomous
Snakes and Their Mimics

Fiction:
The Hunt
Wounded Moon

Nonfiction:
Escape in Iraq:
The Thomas Hamill Story

Photography Credits:
Duane Raver/USFWS: *14, 17, 22, 28*
Timothy Knepp/USFWS: *18, 22, 26*

I dedicate this book to my late father,
Joe W. Bourne III. He is gone from this world,
but never from my heart. Whatever heaven is like,
I hope it includes a lake full of crappie and
a creaky old johnboat so we can relive those
early days of fishing together.
I love you Pa, and I miss you.

CONTENTS

INTRODUCTION

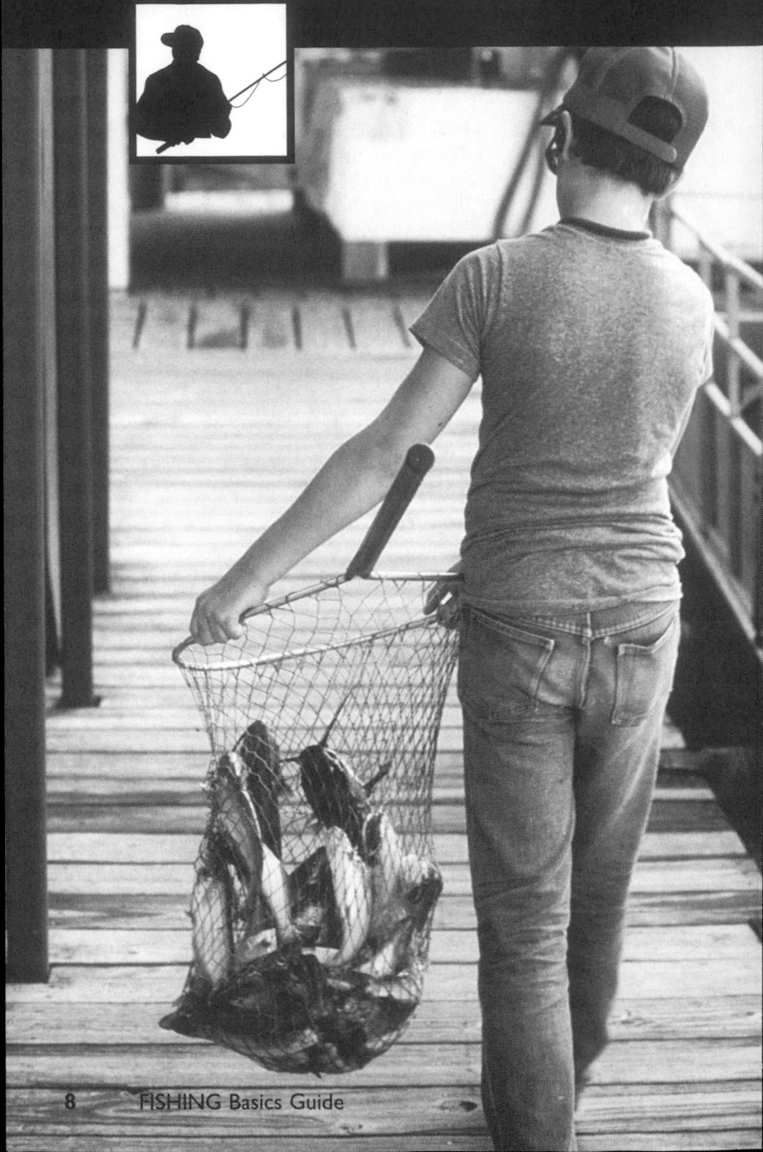

This book will teach you how to catch fish – guaranteed! This is true even if you've never fished before. Or, if you have some fishing experience, this book will help you increase your success. It will help you whether you fish from the bank or from a boat. It will help you if you're male or female, young or old, physically able or disabled. It doesn't matter. If you apply the instructions laid out in this pocket book, and do so persistently, you will catch more and bigger fish – more bass, bluegill, walleye, crappie, catfish, etc. – guaranteed!

How can I make this promise? I can do so because fishing is an undertaking of skill rather than luck. If you increase and sharpen your skills, you will be more successful. Sure, luck sometimes plays a big role in fishing, but nobody's lucky all the time. But if you learn about fish and their habits, if you know where to find them, if you know how to pick the right tackle and baits, and if you learn how to present these baits so they look natural and inviting to the fish, then your odds of success go up. When skill starts replacing luck, your catch rate will certainly begin to rise.

There is an old saying in fishing that 10 percent of the anglers catch 90 percent of the fish. The reverse of this is that 90 percent of the anglers combine to catch only 10 percent of all fish taken on hook and line. The number of experts is small, while the number of beginners and mid-level fishermen is very large. Chances are, if you're reading this book, you are in the 90 percent group, and will profit from the following basic fishing instruction.

Even if you're an accomplished fisherman, it never hurts to go back and review the fundamentals. Sometimes the simplest oversight can cause an otherwise-sound fishing plan to fail. Coaches in all sports start with the basics, and they build successful programs on this foundation.

Why Get Into Fishing?

However, before getting started, why get into fishing? What will you gain by taking up this sport? There are many answers to these questions, because fishing offers different benefits to different people.

For most, it's a healthy, fresh-air activity that can be enjoyed by anybody. Fishing is no discriminator of age, sex or physical skills. Anyone who makes the effort can find a place and a way to catch fish, and experience the pleasures therein!

Fishing provides a perfect setting for fun and togetherness with family and friends. It's amazing how fishing removes barriers between people and allows them to understand and enjoy each other. Fishing is an especially good way for parents to build a strong relationship with children.

Fishing is a good way to make friends. Anglers share a mutual bond and speak a universal language. When two fishermen meet for the first time, they have something in common to talk about.

Fishing is a good way to get back to nature. On the water, the pressures of modern life seem to drift away on the breeze. It's a great way to relax, to tune into the soul-soothing rhythms of the wind and waves.

Fishing offers suspense and excitement. There's great drama in watching a bobber disappear underwater, setting the hook, then battling the fish up to the bank or boat. When you catch a fish, you feel the excitement of a job well done. Fishing provides feelings of accomplishment and self-esteem as you learn the tricks of the sport and how to apply them successfully.

Fishing teaches patience. It teaches perseverance and how to work toward goals. Ponds, lakes and streams can be natural classrooms for some very important lessons in life. And last, fishing can be a source of nutritious, delicious-tasting food. There are few banquets as pleasing as fresh fish that you've caught, cleaned and cooked.

However, there is a warning that should be given regarding this sport! With all its benefits, fishing also carries certain liabilities. It'll hook you just like you plan to hook the fish. It'll cause you to crawl out of bed well before sunrise, travel long distances, burn enormous amounts of energy and even spend large sums of money, all for the chance of tricking a simple fish into biting a bait. For many, fishing is truly addictive.

The Concept of Structure
As you undertake the following study course on fishing, one concept will appear over and over in

regards to locating fish and catching them: the concept of STRUCTURE. I've capitalized this word for emphasis. This is the key to finding fish, which is the first step in getting them to bite.

Here's the idea. Most fish don't just meander randomly through their home water. Instead, they hang around specific, predictable spots most of the time. These are places that have some difference or feature that the fish like or use in their daily lives. In fishing, these differences or features are called "structure."

Let's use a simple example to explain this concept. Say there's a man walking in a desert. If there's nothing but sand, he'll wander aimlessly. But if somebody erects a telephone pole in the middle of that desert, he'll walk straight to it and probably hang around it. The telephone pole gives him a point of reference. Or, say somebody builds a fence across the desert, and the man encounters it. He'll probably turn and follow it. Now he has something to give order to his movements. If the telephone pole I mentioned is somewhere along the fence, this is a likely spot for the man to stop, since this place is different, hence more attractive, compared to the rest of the desert.

Underwater features affect fish the same way. If the bottom is flat and void of any special features, fish will swim around without any pattern. But there's almost always some structure that will attract or guide their movements. Submerged stumps, logs, rocks, weed clumps and other objects are like the telephone pole. They give fish something to orient to. A sunken creek or river channel, a submerged gully or an inundated roadbed is like the fence. Fish will swim along it. A stump or rockpile on the edge of a sunken channel or a bend in the channel is a likely place for a fish to stop and rest as it swims along this structure.

As we proceed into succeeding chapters, remember that structure is anything different from the norm. This applies to ponds, natural lakes, manmade reservoirs, streams and rivers - wherever fish live. Structure can be sunken channels, reefs, bridge foundations, boat docks, manmade fish attractors, an old car sunk in the lake or anything different from a clean, smooth bottom.

Also, structure may be more subtle, such as a spot where the current changes direction, where there is a change in bottom makeup (for instance, where a mud bottom changes into gravel), where muddy water gives way to clear or even where shadows fall onto the water's surface.

The point is, think changes or differences in the fish's environment, and you'll be thinking structure. In later sections of this book, we'll get into a more detailed discussion of how fish relate to structure and how this affects specific fishing techniques.

LARGEMOUTH BASS

SMALLMOUTH BASS

BLUEGILL SUNFISH

BLACK CRAPPIE

WHITE CRAPPIE

Fish are among the most interesting creatures on earth! They come in an amazing variety of species and sizes. They live in virtually all waters where their life basics are available to them. Some are predators; they feed on other fish and aquatic creatures. Others are prey species, spending their lives in danger of being gobbled by larger fish that share their waters.

The first step in learning to catch fish is learning about fish: which species are available, where they can be found and what they eat. The more you know about your target species' behavior, the more likely you are to catch them. Following is a brief look at the freshwater fish species that are most popular with North American anglers.

Black Bass

This group includes three popular species: largemouth bass, smallmouth bass and spotted bass. They are closely related, but differ in spawning habits, life basics and in the waters and foods they prefer.

The largemouth is the most abundant and grows larger than smallmouth or spotted bass. Largemouth live in natural lakes, reservoirs, rivers and ponds from Mexico to Canada and from the East to West Coasts. They feed and rest in quiet, relatively shallow water, and hold around cover such as vegetation, rocks, stumps, brush, etc.

Largemouth bass are predators that eat a wide range of foods. Their primary diet consists of baitfish, crawfish, frogs and insects, but they will also strike ducklings, mice, snakes and virtually any other living creature that they can swallow.

Smallmouth bass prefer clearer, cooler waters. They like a rocky or sandy environment and adapt well to medium-strength currents. Because of these preferences, they thrive in streams, lakes and reservoirs of the Northeast, Midwest and southern Canadian provinces. Also, the Great Lakes support huge smallmouth populations. Smallmouth bass occur naturally as far south as north Alabama and Georgia, and they have been successfully stocked into lakes and rivers west of the Rockies.

Smallmouth bass are feeding opportunists. Their favorite prey are minnows and crawfish, but they will also eat a wide variety of other foods.

Spotted bass ("Kentucky bass") are the third common member of the black bass family. This fish was recognized as a distinct species in 1927.

The spotted bass is an intermediate species between the largemouth and smallmouth both in appearance and habits. Its name comes from rows of small, dark spots running from head to tail below a lateral band of dark-green, diamond-shaped blotches. Spotted bass occur naturally from Texas to Georgia and north up the Mississippi, Ohio and Missouri River drainages. These fish have also been stocked in several western states.

Spotted bass like some current, but not too much. They like deep water, and collect in large schools and chase baitfish in open water. They feed primarily on baitfish, crawfish and insects.

Some lakes contain all three of these black bass

species. Largemouth will be back in the quiet coves. Smallmouth will hold along deep shorelines and main lake reefs; and spotted bass will roam through the open lake in search of prey. Occasionally these three bass species will mix to feed on the same food source.

Spawning habits of black bass species are similar. When water temperature approaches the mid-50° F range, these fish go on feeding binges to build up energy for spawning. Smallmouth and spotted bass begin nesting when the water temperature nears 60°. They establish nests on shorelines or flats, frequently next to a stump, rock, log, etc. that offers shelter. Largemouth prefer 65° water for spawning, and fan their nests in wind-protected areas along the sides or back of lake embayments. Largemouth typically nest in shallower water (2-5 feet on average) than smallmouth or spotted bass.

Sunfish

To biologists, "sunfish" is the family name for several species, including bass, crappie and bluegill. However, to most anglers, "sunfish" is a collective term for bluegill, shellcrackers, pumpkinseeds, green sunfish, longear sunfish, warmouth and other similar species that southerners call "bream." These are the most numerous and widespread of all panfish.

Sunfish live in warm-water lakes, reservoirs, rivers and ponds throughout the U.S. and southern Canada. They spend most time in shallow

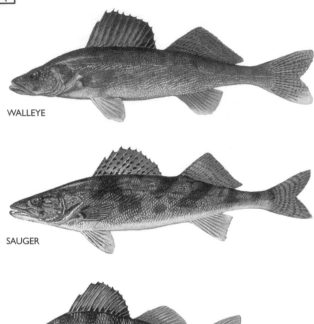

WALLEYE

SAUGER

YELLOW PERCH

MUSKELLUNGE

to medium depths, usually around weeds, rocks, brush, boat docks or other cover types. They feed mostly on tiny invertebrates, larval and adult insects, worms, small minnows and other prey.

Sunfish are capable of reproducing in great numbers. One adult female will produce tens of thousands of eggs in a single season. Because of this, many smaller waters experience sunfish overpopulation. In waters where there are enough bass and other predators to prevent overpopulation, some sunfish species will average a half-pound in size, and some individuals can exceed a pound.

Crappie

Crappie are widespread and abundant in many waters, and are prized for their delicious table quality. They average larger in size than sunfish, and they are fairly easy to catch. There are two crappie species: white and black. Differences between these species are minor. Black crappie have darker, blotchier scale patterns than white crappie, which usually have dark vertical bars.

Both species live in natural lakes, reservoirs, larger ponds and quiet, deep pools of medium-to-large streams. Crappie occur naturally from southern Ontario to the Gulf of Mexico in the eastern half of North America. They have been stocked in numerous lakes and rivers in the West. Black crappie are typically found in cooler, clearer lakes, while white crappie inhabit warmer lakes of dingier color.

Traditionally, most crappie fishing occurs in the

spring, when the fish migrate into quiet, shallow areas to spawn. When the water temperature climbs into the low-60°F range, they begin laying eggs in or next to such cover as reeds, brush, stumps or man-made fish attractors.

After spawning, crappie head back to deeper water, where they collect in schools and hold along sunken creek channels, weed lines, standing timber, sunken brushpiles and other areas where the lake bottom contour changes suddenly or where deep submerged cover exists.

Crappie feed mainly on small baitfish and invertebrates. In some lakes, they average a pound or more in size; crappie over 2 pounds are considered trophies.

Walleye

The walleye is a member of the perch family. It gets its name from its large, glassy, light-sensitive eyes. While walleye average 1-3 pounds, in some waters they grow to more than 20 pounds.

Walleye are native to cool, clean lakes, reservoirs and major rivers of the central United States and much of Canada. They've been stocked in both eastern and western waters outside their home range.

Walleye spend most of their time in deep mainlake/river areas where there is good water circulation, but they also frequently feed on shallow flats and close to shore. They normally move into these areas in low-light periods such as night, dawn, dusk, on cloudy days or when vegetation or muddy water shields them from bright sunlight. A walleye's main food is small baitfish, though it will also feed on insects and small crustaceans and amphibians.

Walleye are early spawners. Their spawning run starts when the water temperature climbs above 45°F. Walleye in lakes spawn on shallow flats with hard, clean bottoms. In rivers, walleye spawn below riffles in pools with rock or sand bottoms. In river-fed lakes and reservoirs, an upstream spawning run is the rule.

A characteristic of these fish, one that beginning anglers should be aware of, is their sharp teeth!

Sauger

Sauger are closely related to walleye, and many people confuse them because of their similar appearance and habits. But there are two easy ways to tell them apart. Sauger have dark, saddle-like blotches on their backs (as opposed to the walleye's smooth golden scale pattern). Also, sauger have dark spots on the main dorsal fin. (A walleye's dorsal fin is spot-free.)

Sauger don't grow as large as walleye and seldom reach 4 pounds. The sauger is a river fish, though it also lives in river impoundments and some natural lakes. Its range includes the Mississippi Valley west of the Appalachian Mountains and north to James Bay in Canada. Sometimes sauger are found co-existing with walleye, but they're more tolerant of dingy water. This means sauger can thrive in slow-moving, silty streams where walleye can't survive.

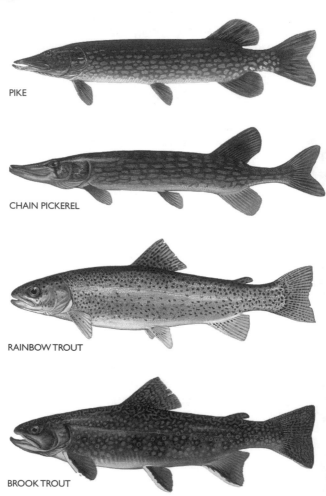

PIKE

CHAIN PICKEREL

RAINBOW TROUT

BROOK TROUT

The sauger's feeding and spawning habits are very similar to those of walleye. This fish is also prized by anglers for its fine table quality. And like walleye, sauger have sharp teeth.

Yellow Perch

Yellow perch are members of the perch family. These fish average 6 -10 inches long. Their natural range extends throughout the Northeast, Midwest and Canada (except British Columbia). These fish live in all of the Great Lakes and inhabit many brackish waters along the Atlantic Coast. Yellow perch have been stocked in numerous reservoirs outside of their natural range.

These fish thrive in clean lakes, reservoirs, ponds and large rivers that have sand, rock or gravel bottoms. They also abound in weedy, mud-bottomed lakes, though these are the type of spots where they tend to run smaller in size.

Yellow perch swim in schools and feed on minnows, small crustaceans and invertebrates. Adults remain in deep water, moving shallow to feed during daylight hours in areas exposed to sunlight.

These fish begin spawning when the water temperature climbs into the mid-40°F range (mid-50s in their southern range). Yellow perch often make spawning runs up feeder streams; they also spawn around shallow weeds and brush.

Muskellunge

Many anglers view the "muskie" as the supreme

freshwater trophy fish. Muskies are top predators and are never very numerous in any body of water. They are capable of growing huge in size.

The muskie is a member of the pike family. It is found in natural lakes, reservoirs and streams/rivers in the Northeast, upper Midwest and southern Canada. This fish requires cool, clean water.

The muskie is cylinder-shaped, with a long, powerful body. Its sides are yellow-tined and marked with dark blotches or bars. This fish has a flat, duck-like mouth and very sharp teeth! It feeds mainly on smaller fish, but it will also attack birds, muskrats and other creatures that enter its domain.

Muskies typically stalk their prey in shallow water, around reeds, rocky shoals, quiet eddy pools and other similar spots. During warm months, they feed more in low-light periods of dawn and dusk. On cloudy days, however, they may feed anytime. Muskies live many years and frequently grow beyond 35 pounds. The muskie is a late spawner (water temperature in the mid-50°F range).

Northern Pike

Members of the pike family, "northerns" are much more numerous than muskies, and they are easier to catch. By nature, pike are very aggressive, and they often attack any bright, flashy lure.

Pike inhabit natural lakes, reservoirs, rivers and streams throughout the northeastern and north-central U. S. and most of Canada. They thrive in warm, shallow lakes or river sloughs with an abundance of water weeds.

The pike's body is shaped like a muskie's: long and round with the same flat, pointed mouth and sharp teeth. Its color is dark olive on the sides with light, wavy spots. Its belly is white. Pike can grow over 20 pounds.

Pike spawn in quiet, shallow areas when the water temperature climbs into the 40°F range. After spawning, they linger around weedbeds, especially those close to underwater contour changes. Most of the pike's diet consists of fish.

Pickerel

These toothy predators are a mini-version of pike and muskies. Their sides are covered with a yellowish chain pattern on a green background. Most pickerel range from 1-3 pounds, but can grow larger than this in southern habitats.

The grass and redfin pickerels rarely reach a foot in length. The redfin is found along the Atlantic coastal plain in small creeks and shallow ponds. The grass pickerel's range is primarily in the Mississippi and Great Lakes drainages.

Pickerel spawn in shallow weeds as water temperatures reach the high 40°F range. They are active in cold water.

Trout

Several trout species inhabit North America and are important sportfish. They live in many types of waters, from small brooks to huge lakes. Some

LAKE TROUT

CUTTHROAT TROUT

COHO SALMON

trout are natives; others are raised in hatcheries and released into suitable waters. Trout are cold-water fish and lively fighters when hooked.

The U. S. and Canada have five major trout species: rainbows, German browns, brook trout, cutthroats and lake trout. Six other species found in localized areas are Apache trout, Arctic char, bull trout, Dolly Vardens, Gila trout and golden trout.

Rainbows are named for the pink streak down their sides. Native to western states, this fish has been stocked in streams, ponds and lakes through-out much of the U. S. and lower Canada.

The German brown trout has been widely stocked in American waters. These fish have dark or orange spots on their sides. They are wary and difficult to catch and tolerate slightly higher water temperatures than other trout.

Brook trout are native to the eastern U. S. and Canada and have been transplanted to other areas. They have light, wormlike markings along their backs with small blue and red dots along their sides.

Cutthroat trout are found mainly in the western U. S. and Canada. Their name comes from the red markings behind and under the lower jaw. Their sides are dotted with small black spots.

Lake trout are what their name implies: residents of large, cold-water lakes from Canada south through the Canadian shield lakes of northern and Midwestern states. Lake trout also live in many western lakes. They are silver-gray in color, and they have deeply-forked tails.

WHITE BASS

STRIPED BASS

FLATHEAD CATFISH

BULLHEAD CATFISH

Trout feed on a broad variety of larval and adult insects, minnows, worms and crustaceans. In streams, trout spawn in shallow riffles where they build nests (or "redds") in gravel.

Salmon

Pacific salmon were first stocked into the Great Lakes in the late 1960s. The Chinook salmon is the largest species, reaching more than 30 pounds. Coho salmon run smaller, but 20-pounders aren't uncommon. Sockeye and pink salmon are smaller and less common.

These open-water predators feed on deep-swimming schools of alewives and smelt, but will also feed near the surface. Coho salmon mature in three years before returning to the stream where they were stocked or hatched. Chinooks grow for an extra year before returning to their stream of origin, where they die after spawning.

White Bass

White bass are natives of the Great Lakes and the Mississippi River system and have been widely stocked beyond this range. The white bass has silvery-white sides with dark stripes running from the gills back to the tail.

Early each spring, white bass make spawning runs up river and reservoir tributaries. After they spawn, white bass move back into deep pools in rivers and open water in reservoirs. Small shad are the white bass' main food source.

Stripers

"Striper" and "rockfish" are two nicknames for the saltwater striped bass. Native to the Atlantic Ocean and Gulf of Mexico, this fish can also live in freshwater, and it's been stocked extensively in rivers and large reservoirs throughout the mid- and western-United States. It does best where water temperature doesn't exceed 75°F.

Stripers look like large white bass, except they are more elongated, and they grow huge in size. They are open-water fish, roving in schools through main-lake and river areas in search of prey.

Catfish

Catfish live in warm-water rivers, ponds, lakes and reservoirs throughout much of the U.S. and southern Canada. There are three common American catfish species: channel catfish, blue catfish and flathead catfish.

Channel catfish have olive-blue sides fading to silver-white bellies, with small dark spots on their backs and sides. Channel cats live mostly in rivers or lakes with slow to moderate currents. They are the smallest of the three catfish species, rarely exceeding 25 pounds.

Blue catfish look very much like channels, except without spots on their backs and sides. They grow larger than channel catfish, occasionally exceeding 100 pounds and thrive in big, slow-moving rivers.

Flathead catfish are so-named because of their appearance. The flathead's mouth is long and flat, and its lower jaw is slightly longer than its upper jaw. Its back and sides are mottled brown with a lighter belly. They prefer current and clean water.

All three of these species share certain traits. They have a slick, scaleless skin and have eight barbels (whiskers) around the mouth.

Blue and channel catfish eat worms, insects, baitfish, crawfish and invertebrates. Flatheads feed primarily on live foods — baitfish, crawfish, etc. They feed mainly on the bottom, though they will move up and forage near the surface.

Catfish spawn in late spring, after the water temperature reaches 70°F. Females lay eggs in holes in the bank, under logs or in other spots that offer protection from current and concealment from predators.

Bullheads

There are three species of bullheads in North America: black, brown and yellow. Their range covers most of the United States and southern Canada. They live in a variety of waters, from small ponds and marshes to large impoundments and rivers. Three other species (snail, spotted and flat bullhead) are found in the Southeast. Bullheads prefer quiet, warm waters, and hang close to bottom. They rarely grow larger than 2 pounds.

2. FINDING GOOD FISHING SPOTS

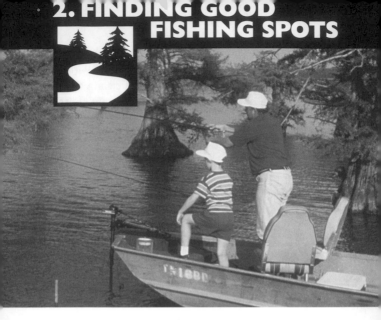

My favorite way to fish is to paddle a canoe or wade along a free-running stream, casting a crawfish lure for smallmouth, spotted bass and other small sunfish. This type of fishing is simple. It's very relaxing. The setting is usually beautiful, and stream fish typically bite with little hesitation. All these things combine for a wonderful outing.

Still, for reasons I don't understand, most anglers overlook streams and the light tackle methods I enjoy. Many are more attuned to big waters, fast boats and run-and-gun tactics. The main reason streams offer good fishing is because they don't get much fishing pressure.

Really extraordinary fishing spots are a rare find,

but it's not difficult for beginning anglers to locate first-rate places where they can expect reasonable success, or better. The U. S. and Canada teem with good fishing holes, and many of them are open to the public. Besides streams, you can find fish in natural lakes, man-made reservoirs, swamps, rivers, farm ponds, beaver ponds, oxbow lakes, drainage canals, tailraces below dams, mining pits, city lakes, pay lakes, coastal marshes and other spots. Some of these places already get plenty of fishing pressure but others await someone to discover them.

As you learn more about fishing, you should also start looking for places where you can go fishing. Make a list of possibilities, and research them thoroughly to learn which ones are best. Doing this is a matter of knowing where to look, whom to ask and what information to collect. I guarantee there is a broad range of fishing waters close to where you live, wherever you live!

Following is a step-by-step guide for finding good fishing holes anywhere in North America.

Beginning the Search

Locating good fishing spots is like being a detective and unraveling a mystery. Collect as much information as possible from many different sources, then compare notes to see which spots seem to be best. How good are they? How accessible are they? How much fishing pressure do they get?

Many government agencies can provide information about public fishing spots. These include state fish and wildlife agencies, tourism bureaus, city recreation departments, utility companies, public resource agencies and military reservations. Virtually all these agencies have web sites that list public fishing opportunities.

To start your search, log onto the web site www.recreation.gov. This site provides a state-by-state listing of all federal lands where public recreation is available. (Examples include federal reservoirs, national forests, national parks, national wildlife refuges, etc.) It also provides links to state agency web sites that will have their own wealth of information about fishing opportunities.

Another way to find fishing spots on-line is to go to a search engine (www.google.com) and type in "Fishing in _____", filling your state in the blank. You'll come up with thousands of leads.

Those who don't have Internet access can use the telephone and mail to obtain information. Call your state fish and wildlife agency. Check in your public library for a list of government agencies, then call them and ask for the public information or recreation branch.

When you're browsing web sites or talking to an information contact, try to obtain the following:

- A list of public fishing spots near your home, and brochures, maps and other details about these potential locations.
- The name, phone number and e-mail address of the biologist who manages these fisheries.

- The names, phone numbers and e-mail addresses of fish/wildlife officers who patrol the spots on the list.
- Any brochures listing fishing seasons, license requirements, creel limits and other pertinent regulations.

Sometimes biologists can provide detailed information about specific fisheries, or a biologist might know of another overlooked opportunity you can try. Don't be hesitant about calling a biologist who works for a public agency. Biologists are usually eager to help people enjoy the benefits of their fisheries' management efforts.

The same is true for wildlife officers. These men and women spend much of their lives in the field, and they will probably know how good the fishing is in a lake/stream/pond in which you're interested.

Bait and Tackle Shops, Other Info Sources

Local bait and tackle shops can be an excellent source of information for finding good fishing. Bait shop operators talk to fishermen everyday, and make it their business to keep up with what is biting, and where. Also, it's in their best interest to provide you with information to help you catch fish. By doing so, they are creating another customer. This is why you can usually trust the advice you get in a bait/tackle store.

Another helpful source is the outdoor writer at your local newspaper. Tell him you're a beginner looking for a good place to go fishing. In essence, contact anybody you can think of who has any connection to fishing.

Don't overlook books, maps or pamphlets containing information about fishing in your area. Books and phamphlets are often available that contain a wealth of information. Look for such printed material in libraries, bookstores and bait shops.

Fishing on Private Lands

While most of the advice above applies to public fishing waters, many excellent spots exist on private land. These include stock ponds, watershed lakes, irrigation ditches and reservoirs. Permission to fish private waters may not be easy to obtain, but there's no harm in asking.

Of course, such permission comes with the responsibility to show respect for the landowner and his property. Don't forget, you're his guest. Never litter his property. If a gate is closed, don't leave it open, if open, don't close it. Don't climb over wire fences and ride them down. Don't drive off established roads or damage crops. Always offer to share what you catch. If you act responsibly and don't abuse your privilege, you will probably be welcomed to fish there again.

Pay Lakes and Fishing Piers

One special opportunity for beginning anglers is pay lakes and fishing piers. These are commercial fishing establishments that are run for profit. At some places you pay a flat rate per hour of fishing. At others, you pay by the pound for fish you catch.

Rating Your Fishing Spots

After compiling a list of possible fishing spots, it's time to rate them. There are several criteria for doing so. How far away are they, and how difficult to reach? How much fishing pressure do they receive? If you don't have a boat, can you fish from the bank, bridge or pier? Is wade-fishing a possibility? If you have a boat, is a ramp or launch site available?

Next comes the fun part — test-fishing your top prospects to see how good they really are. I recommend test-fishing a new spot at least three times before writing it off. The first time, the fish might not be biting. But when you return, they might be actively feeding. If a particular lake, stream or pond is recommended by biologists, wildlife officers or other reputable sources, don't give up on it too soon.

Over the seasons, as you explore more and more, you will add to your list of fishing places, and you can upgrade continually. When you discover a good new spot, you can discard a marginal one. In a few seasons, you will have a repertoire of favorites where you can go and fish with confidence of catching something.

3. SAFETY IN FISHING

Overall, fishing is a very safe sport, but it does involve certain hazards. Some of these may be life-threatening, others only discomforting. The old adage "an ounce of prevention is worth a pound of cure" applies. Following is a look at safety considerations in fishing, at dangers which can arise and how to avoid or deal with them. We'll take them in order of seriousness: life-threatening first, then discomforting second.

Weather Perils of Fishing

Lightning – Because fishing is an outdoor sport, you will experience different types of weather. This means that sooner or later you'll be exposed to one of the most dangerous of all natural killers: lightning. Lightning doesn't get the scare publicity that tornadoes, hurricanes and other sensational weather phenomena do. But each year lightning claims more lives than all other weather-related accidents combined. Invariably, some of these victims are fishermen.

Kids learn at an early age that lightning strikes tall objects. Tallness is relative. A fisherman in a boat on a lake is tall in comparison to what's around him. The same is true about an angler standing on a flat, barren shoreline. In either case, if the fisherman is using a rod (particularly graphite), in effect he's holding a lightning rod, and he's certainly inviting disaster.

The cardinal rule is never allow yourself to get caught where lightning is likely to strike. If you see a storm coming, get off the water or away from high areas or tall objects. The safest place to be is inside a house or vehicle. Don't stand under isolated trees or poles. If you get caught in an electrical storm, wait it out in the lowest spot you can find, and keep a low profile.

High winds – High winds are another weather peril for anglers in boats. If you think the waves are too high, don't go out. If you are out and see a storm coming, head in. If you get caught in high waves and start taking water, don't try to get back to the dock or ramp. Turn and go with the wind.

If your boat swamps, stay in it. Most boats have level flotation, and even if they fill with water, they won't sink. Keep your life jacket cinched tightly, try to stay calm and wait for rescue.

Fog – Sometimes you may be tempted to head out onto a foggy lake. My advice is don't go. When you can't see where you're going, you risk running into an unseen object or getting lost. Stay at the boat ramp until the fog lifts. You won't miss much fishing, and won't be taking risks. Also, keep a GPS or a compass handy in case fog rolls in. Fog causes you to lose all sense of direction, and a GPS or compass can help you find your way.

Hypothermia – Exposure is the common term for hypothermia. This is a loss of body heat – typically caused by getting wet – that can eventually cause death. This is not just a winter problem. It can occur in other seasons, too. It's usually brought on by a combination of cool air, wind and wet clothes. Evaporation causes a rapid heat loss, and this leads to a drop in body temperature.

The first sign of hypothermia is mild shivering. This is the body's way of trying to warm itself, and it's also a warning signal of trouble. If something isn't done to reverse this situation, the shivering can become uncontrollable, and the victim starts losing feeling in his arms and legs. His speech becomes slurred, and his thinking gets fuzzy. If his body temperature continues to drop (75-80°F), he will slip into a coma and possibly die.

If you start shivering, don't ignore this signal! There are two things to do: remove the cause of cooling (wet clothing); and restore body heat. This can be done by replacing wet clothes with dry ones, drinking warm fluids, eating energy-rich foods and by warming next to a fire or other heat source. You must stop the loss of body heat and restore it to a normal level. If the symptoms progress to uncontrollable shivering, get medical help fast. Remember, hypothermia is a killer.

The Danger of Drowning

Drowning is a constant danger to fishermen. Each year we hear tragic stories of anglers who have fallen out of boats or off the bank and were lost. This danger is easily avoided. Following are commonsense rules for making sure you won't become a drowning victim.

Wear a life preserver. – Using a life preserver is the "ounce of prevention" I mentioned earlier. Very few anglers drown while wearing a Coast Guard-approved personal flotation device (PFD). Whenever you're in a boat, you're required to have such a preserver with you. You're not required to wear it, however, and this gets many lackadaisical fishermen in trouble.

Accidents happen when you least expect them, and they happen quickly. If you're not wearing your life preserver, and your boat suddenly overturns, you probably won't have a chance to put your PFD on. Always wear your PFD when the boat is running, and zip it up or tie it. Also, it's a good idea to wear it even when the boat's not running, especially if you're a poor swimmer. A vest-type preserver isn't bulky. It's comfortable, and it won't interfere with your fishing.

A better option may be an approved inflatable-type PFD that's worn like suspenders. If you fall out of the boat, a quick tug on a lanyard activates a CO_2 cartridge that instantly inflates the PFD.

Bank fishermen should also consider wearing a PFD. Especially if you're fishing along steep banks, tailraces, docks, bridges or similar spots. Children should never be allowed close to such spots without wearing a securely fastened PFD.

Don't overload the boat. – Never put too much load into too small a boat. Little boats aren't meant for heavy loads, especially when there's a chance of encountering high waves, strong current, etc. This lesson absolutely applies to all fishermen and other boaters. Always be certain that your boat is seaworthy enough to handle rough water.

All boats are rated for maximum loads. Before you leave shore, figure the total weight that will be carried in the boat, and don't overload it. Also, be certain that you distribute the weight evenly throughout the boat.

Don't drink and boat. – The statistics tell a sad story. A majority of boating accidents involve alcohol consumption. Drinking and boating is just as serious as drinking and driving. (Many states now have laws against the former.) The bottom line is, don't drink and boat!

Avoid known danger areas. – Tailwaters, dam intakes, rapids, waterfalls and other areas with strong currents or underwater objects pose special dangers to fishermen. Never fish where posted warnings or your commonsense tells you it's unsafe. Be alert to sudden water releases when fishing below dams. After a hard rain, avoid streams prone to flash flooding.

Avoid unsafe ice when ice-fishing. – Each fall a few anglers go out on new ice too early, or try to stretch the spring season by fishing on ice that is thawing and rotten. Incidents of fishermen breaking through thin ice and drowning are all too common and could be avoided if anglers would learn to be more cautious.

Here's the rule to follow: two inches of new, clean ice is safe to walk on. Anything less is dangerous. Also, don't walk on ice when you see air bubbles or cracks. When walking on new ice, have a partner follow a few feet behind, or you follow him! The person walking behind should carry a length of rope or a long pole to pull his partner out if he breaks through the ice. Take a long-handle chisel and tap in front of you to make sure the ice is solid. But again, if there's any reasonable question that the ice is unsafe, don't go out on it!

Veteran ice fishermen wear PFDs when walking on ice and carry long nails or pointed dowels in a handy pocket. If you break through, these can be used to jab into ice at the edge of the hole in order to gain a grip to pull yourself out.

The Danger of Flying Hooks

There are three times when hooks fly: when you're casting (or when your buddy is casting); when you or he snatches a hung-up lure out of a shoreside limb; when you or he is fishing with a surface lure, and you set the hook and miss. These "flying" hooks can be hazardous to anglers who happen to be in their path. Be alert when you're casting, and also when others are casting. If your bait snags on a bush or limb, don't get impatient and yank. Try to flip your bait out, and if it won't come, go get it.

Sunglasses or clear safety glasses will protect your eyes from flying hooks. I wear sunglasses during daytime fishing, and I wear safety glasses when night-fishing. I particularly enjoy night-fishing with topwater lures for bass. Most strikes, however, are heard instead of seen. If the fish misses the lure, and you rear back with your rod, you've got a hook-studded missile flying at you through the dark.

HOW TO REMOVE EMBEDDED HOOKS

Barb buried in

Line around wrist

Despite your best prevention efforts, sooner or later you or your fishing partner will likely be on the receiving end of a flying hook, or you'll sit or step on a hook. When this happens, you have a choice. You can go to a doctor and have it surgically removed, or you can pull the hook out yourself by the following method, which is simple and fairly painless.

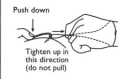

Push down

Tighten up in this direction (do not pull)

You'll need two 18-inch pieces of strong twine. (Monofilament doubled over works well.) If the embedded hook is attached to a lure, remove the lure so only the hook remains. Run one piece of twine through the eye (hole) of the hook, and hold it snug against the skin. With the other hand, loop the other piece of twine through the bend of the hook (between the skin and the hook), pull out all slack, and get a strong grip. If you are doing this properly, the two pieces of string will be pulling in opposite directions.

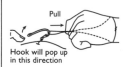

Pull

Hook will pop up in this direction

Now, hold the hook eye firmly in place next to the skin. With the other string, yank up and away very suddenly and forcefully. Done properly, this yields a fulcrum movement that pops the barb back out the entry hole. Wash the puncture wound, treat it with antiseptic and apply a Band-Aid, then go back fishing. Watch closely the next few days for any sign of infection, and if any appears, seek medical attention.

A basic fishing outfit has four components: a pole (or rod/reel), line, a terminal rig (hooks, sinkers, floats) and some type of bait — live or artificial. Various combinations of these components can be used to catch most species. The trick, however, comes in selecting the right combination for the type and size fish you're targeting, with the fishing method and bait you plan to use.

A good way to think about your tackle is as a set of "fishing tools." Various tackle items have specific purposes. You wouldn't choose a hammer to saw a board in two, and you shouldn't select a heavy bass outfit to go after bluegill. Instead, you must learn to match the right "fishing tool" to the "job" you wish to do. Anglers who do this will be much more effective than others who pick the wrong "tools."

The Pole or Rod

A beginner should start with one multi-purpose fishing rod/reel combo that can be used for several situations. As you get more involved in fishing, you'll probably want more specialized tackle. But when you're getting started, your first outfit should be simple and inexpensive, yet versatile enough to catch many different species of fish.

Differences Between Poles and Rods

Mechanically, a fishing pole or rod is a lever that serves as an extension of the angler's arm. With either, you get more length and leverage for presenting a bait, setting a hook and battling and landing a fish.

Poles are longer than rods. Poles aren't meant for casting, however, the line is instead fixed to the end of the pole and the bait is presented by swinging the line. Rods, on the other hand, are shorter than poles, and are fitted with a reel to hold the line.

How you fish determines whether you need a pole or a rod. If you're going after bluegill close to the bank, a pole may be best. But if you're trying for bass away from shore, or if you're fishing in deep water for walleye, you need a rod and reel to get extra casting distance or depth.

Rods/reels are far more versatile than poles because of their reach. They can be used in many more fishing situations. Also, rods may substitute for poles in some close-in fishing situations.

Poles

Poles come in three main materials: natural cane, fiberglass and graphite. They are sold in various lengths, typically from 8 feet to 16 feet - or longer! Some poles are stiff and strong (heavy action) for catfish and other large fish. Other poles are limber (light action) for catching small panfish.

Cane poles are the simplest and least expensive. However, fiberglass and graphite poles are more durable and sensitive to delicate bites, and they offer more features. Many of these poles are collapsible and easy to transport.

Some poles come with a line holder, which allows an angler to change the length of line he's using. One type line holder is a simple reel that mounts on the pole's butt. Another type is a metal bracket around which excess line is wrapped. Poles with line holders usually have guides, or the line is run through a hollow pole and out a hole in the tip. In either case, the reel or line holder on a pole is meant simply for adjusting line length, not casting.

Rods

Buying a rod is more complicated than buying a pole, since there are many more factors to consider. Rods come in different designs (casting, spinning), materials, lengths, actions and handle and guide components. They are sold in a broad range of prices, from inexpensive to very expensive. All these variables can be confusing.

However, there is one simple way to avoid making a bad decision: seek the advice of an experienced angler. This may be the salesman in an outdoor store or tackle department. Tell him what type of fishing you want to do – species, methods, locations and he should be able to outfit you.

Rod Features

Following are brief looks at the different features of fishing rods. Having a basic understanding will help you select a rod that best suits your needs.

Rod type – Rods are designed to match different types of reels. There are four basic types of reels: baitcasting, spinning, spin-cast and fly. Casting rods are designed for use with baitcasting or spin-cast reels. Spinning rods are used with spinning reels, and fly-rods are designed for use with fly-reels. Each type rod has its special uses and advantages/disadvantages.

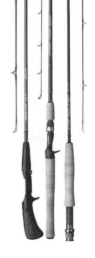

Left to right: Pistol-grip casting rod, standard-grip casting rod, and fly rod.

Length – Most fishing rods measure 5-7 feet long, though highly specialized rods may be shorter or longer. Long rods offer more leverage. They can generally cast farther, but they are harder to cast accurately. Short rods offer less leverage and casting distance, but they are more accurate for close-in casting. Best overall rod lengths for general fishing purposes are $5\frac{1}{2}$ -$6\frac{1}{2}$ feet.

Action – Action refers to a rod's stiffness and how this stiffness is built into the design of the rod. A rod's action has a direct effect on the size of bait a rod can cast effectively and the size fish it can handle. Standard rod actions are: ultralight, light, medium-light, medium, medium-heavy and heavy.

Ultralight rods are very limber. They are best for casting little baits (for example, $\frac{1}{32}$-oz.) for smaller fish. Heavy-action rods are extremely stiff and powerful. They are best for casting heavy baits ($\frac{1}{2}$-1 ounce-plus) and catching such fish as trophy bass, stripers and big catfish. The stiffer the rod the more difficult it is to cast light, small baits. On the other hand, the lighter a rod's action, the less well-suited it is for casting heavy baits. It is crucial to match rod action, line size and bait size.

Mid-weight rods – Light, medium-light and medium – are the most versatile and usually the best choice for beginning fishermen. With a 6-foot medium-light rod, you can land everything from bass and catfish to walleye, white bass, crappie, pike and other species. You need a heavy-action rod only when going after muskies, trophy pike, stripers or the biggest bass in the thickest cover.

One-piece/Multi-piece – Most rods are constructed in one long piece. However, others are made in two or more pieces that can be joined. One-piece rods are stronger and more sensitive, though multi-piece rods provide adequate strength and sensitivity for most situations. The main advantage of a multi-piece rod is convenience in storing and carrying.

Materials – Most modern fishing rods are made from fiberglass, graphite or a combination of these two materials. Fiberglass rods are flexible yet durable. Their drawback is that fiberglass rods weigh more. Also, fiberglass rods are less sensitive to light bites than graphite rods. Conversely, graphite rods are lighter and more sensitive. Their drawbacks are higher cost and brittleness.

Handles – Rod handles come in a range of designs and materials. Some anglers like straight handles; others prefer a pistol-grip. Many rods have long handles that facilitate two-hand casting and extra support when fighting a big fish. Materials vary from cork to plastic or foam.

Casting, Spinning or Fly Tackle

When shopping for a new outfit, should you choose casting, spinning or fly tackle? Again, this choice depends on how you plan to fish and the type and size fish you will target.

Let's start with casting tackle. Casting rods match up with baitcasting and spin-cast reels. Baitcasting reels, also called open face and revolving spool reels, mount on top of the rod in front of the handle. When bait is cast out, its weight pulls line off the reel's exposed spool. Thumb pressure on the spool is used to slow the bait and stop the cast at the desired distance.

Spin-cast reels, also called push-button reels, have a spool that is enclosed inside a hood covering the front of the reel. Line plays out through a small hole in front of the hood. To make a cast, an angler pushes and holds the thumb button down, makes a back-cast, then releases the button during the forward cast. With the button released, the line plays out smoothly. The user then pushes the thumb button again to stop the cast.

Casting rods and these two reel types are normally stronger than spinning reels, and they are used with heavier line and baits for bigger fish. Baitcasting outfits are the most accurate type of casting tackle.

Spinning reels hang under the rod on a straight handle. These reels have an exposed spool and a revolving bail that spins around as the handle is turned, thereby wrapping line around the spool. For casting, the angler catches and holds the line on his forefinger, the bail is tripped out of the way, and the line is released during the forward portion of the cast. The line coils off the spool with almost no resistance. This allows anglers to use spinning tackle to cast very small baits or lures.

Spinning tackle is routinely used by anglers who go after smaller panfish.

Fly-rods/reels are the epitome of specialty fishing. Fly-fishing tackle is used to cast small dry flies, artificial nymphs, streamers (wet flies), popping bugs and other baits that imitate insects, small larvae, etc. These flies and bugs weigh next to nothing, so it's impossible to cast them with casting or spinning tackle. In fact, in fly-casting, the angler uses the weight of the line (rather than the lure) to achieve casting distance. He false casts while letting out more line through the rod's guides. When he has enough line out to reach his target, he completes his cast by driving forward with the rod and allowing the line to settle on the water. The fly or bug just happens to be tagging along on the end of the line on a clear, thin tippet.

Fly-fishing will frequently take fish when casting and spinning techniques are doomed to failure. This is because fly-fishing allows anglers to match the hatch when fish are feeding on tiny insects and larvae.

Fishing Line

Fishing line is the actual link between angler and fish. Anglers must choose the right line for their particular tackle and method, and they must know how to care for their line so it will last longer.

There are two basic types of line available: monofilament and superlines. Monofilament, an extruded nylon line, is a good choice for many fishing situations. It comes in a wide range of break strengths, called pound test. (A 6-pound test line will break when put under 6 pounds of pressure.)

Monofilament lines have some stretch, are abrasion resistant and very sensitive in terms of feel. They come in a variety of colors and a good rule is to match line and water color.

Superlines are a braid of thin, gel-spun polyethylene fibers. Some superlines are fused (the braided fibers are welded together). Other superlines are non-fused, but they all have similar qualities. Superlines are much stronger than monofilament. They have almost no stretch and are limp and extremely sensitive in feel. Their smaller diameter allows for longer casts and they run diving baits deeper.

Which size line is best? Several factors go into this answer. First, tackle must be balanced. Use light line with light tackle and heavier line with heavy tackle. As a general rule, 4-8 lb. test line is best for panfish like bluegill, crappie and walleye. For average-size bass, catfish, pike and similar-sized species, use 8-12 lb. test. For the biggest of these species, or when fishing in heavy weeds or snags, 15-25 lb. test line might be appropriate.

The Concept of Balanced Tackle

One of the most important things to remember in buying tackle is to balance the components of your outfit. Balanced tackle casts and retrieves lures/baits better and plays fish better than unbalanced tackle.

Large sturdy reels are a good match for a heavy-action rods. Other small, light reels should

ROUND BAIT
CASTING

LOW PROFILE BAIT
CASTING

SPIN-CAST

SPINNING

FLY

be mated with light action rods. This is true with baitcasting, spin-cast and spinning tackle.

The same concept applies to line. Heavy-action outfits work best with 15 lb. test or heavier line. Medium-action tackle matches well with line in the 10-15 lb. test range. Light-action tackle should be spooled with 4-8 lb. test line. Ultra-light tackle works best with 2-6 lb. test line. (These line weights pertain to monofilament. If a superline is preferred, select one with a diameter that corresponds to the appropriate pound test size. 30 lb. test superline may have the same diameter as 12 lb. test monofilament.)

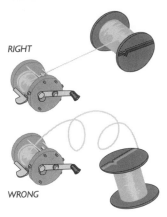

RIGHT

WRONG

The final component in balancing tackle is the lure. It's very practical to cast a $\frac{1}{16}$-oz. lure on an ultra-light outfit spooled with 4lb. test line. Conversely, it's impossible to cast a $\frac{1}{16}$-oz. lure on heavy-action tackle. Use light-action tackle for light lures (up to $\frac{1}{8}$ oz.), and heavy-action tackle to cast heavy lures ($\frac{1}{2}$ oz. or heavier).

Adding Line Onto a Reel

Spooling line onto a reel must be done correctly. Improper spooling can lead to backlashes, loss of casting distance, line twist and other nuisances.

To spool line onto a baitcasting reel, run the line through the tip guide, then through all rod guides to the reel. Run the line through the reel's level wind (the guide that feeds line on/off the reel). Loop the line around the reel spool and tie it on with a line end knot. Snug the line tightly to the spool, and clip the tag end. Have a friend hold the line in front of the rod tip, and run a pencil through the spool so it will turn freely and crank line onto the reel. Hold the rod tip up and keep slight pressure on the line so it goes on the reel spool uniformly, within a quarter inch of the top of the spool.

With a spin-cast reel, run the line through the rod guides. Unscrew the reel hood, poke the line through the hole in the center, tie it around the reel spool with a line end knot and replace the hood. Reel on line until it is an $^1/_8$-inch from the outside edge of the spool.

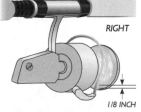

RIGHT

1/8 INCH

With a spinning reel, run the line through the rod guides. Open the bail (flip it down), tie the line on with a line end knot and close the bail. Lay the filler spool on the floor so line will coil off in the same direction the reel spool turns. With a right-hand reel, the spool will turn clockwise, so lay the filler spool on the side that allows line to come off clockwise. This prevents line twist. Add line to within a quarter-inch of the edge of the reel spool.

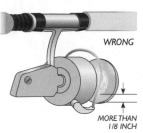

WRONG

MORE THAN 1/8 INCH

Tying Line Onto a Pole

Tie the line onto the pole 18 inches down from the tip. Then wrap line around the pole candy-cane style to the tip, and tie it again. Adjust the line to whatever length line is desired, and clip it off. The line should be approximately the same length as the pole, or slightly shorter.

5. BASIC FISHING RIGS

A fishing rig is whatever you tie on the end of your line to hold and present your bait. It's a combination of hooks, sinkers, floats, snaps, swivels, leaders and the knots that tie everything together.

Fishermen use many different rigs for special fishing situations. There are rigs for live bait and artificial lures. There are rigs for fishing on the bottom, on the surface and in between. There are rigs for trolling, drifting and staying in one spot. There are rigs for fishing in current and still water. There are rigs for using more than one bait at a time. Beginners don't need to learn a lot of complicated rigs, for now, a few basic rigs will provide the means for catching most popular species in many settings.

Fishing Knots:
Holding the Rig Together

One thing all fishing rigs have in common is knots, so learning to tie knots is the logical starting point in a discussion of rigs. You will have to tie knots several times on each fishing trip, so learn this lesson well!

Tying a knot in a fishing line weakens it. An improperly tied knot can reduce line strength by more than 50 percent. But a properly tied knot will retain up to 95 percent of line strength.

Following are instructions for tying six fundamental knots. The first three are used for tying line to hooks, sinkers, swivels, etc. The fourth knot is used to tie a loop in the line. The fifth knot is the one I use to tie two lines together when I'm adding line to my reel. And the sixth is a good knot for adding line to an empty reel spool.

When tying any of these knots, I always follow two rules: before snugging a knot tight, I always spit on it to lubricate it. Saliva reduces line-weakening friction and heat buildup as the knot draws tight. And I always leave $1/8$ inch of line when I clip the tag end. This allows for some slippage in the knot without it coming undone.

Trilene knot – This is the knot I use for 90 pecent of my fishing. I tie it almost

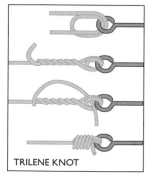

TRILENE KNOT

every time I need a line-to-hook or line-to-lure connection. It's a very strong knot, and it takes only a small amount of practice to master. I highly recommend it.

To tie the Trilene knot, run approximately 4 inches of line through the hook eye, loop it around and pass it through the hook eye again. Pull the line to draw the loop down to a small diameter (¼-½inch). Now catch and hold this loop between your thumb and forefinger to keep it open. Wrap the end of the line around the standing line 5 times. Last, pass the end back through the loop, and snug the knot tight by pulling the standing line and the hook in opposite directions. Trim the tag end.

Palomar knot – This general-purpose knot offers maximum strength and versatility. The palomar knot is dependable and easy to tie, and is a good alternative to the Trilene knot.

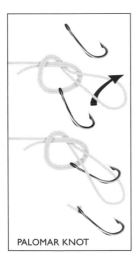

PALOMAR KNOT

To tie the palomar, bend the line back on itself to form a double strand 6 inches long. Pass this double strand through the hook eye, and tie a loose overhand knot, leaving a loop deep enough so the hook or lure can pass through it. Pass the hook through the loop, then tighten the knot by pulling the hook with one hand

and the double strand of line with the other. Trim the tag end.

Improved clinch knot – This is a third general-purpose knot. It's slightly weaker than the Trilene or palomar knot, but is strong and easy enough to tie to be the choice of many experts.

To tie the improved clinch knot, thread the line through the hook eye 3-4 inches.

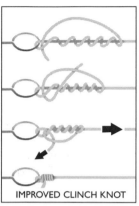

IMPROVED CLINCH KNOT

Wrap the end of the line around the standing line 6 times. Then run the end back through the opening between the hook and the first wrap. Last, turn the end up and thread it through the long loop between the wraps and the downturned line. Hold the end and snug the line by pulling the standing line and hook in opposite directions. Clip the tag end.

Surgeon's loop – When you want to tie a loop in your line, this is the knot to use. The surgeon's loop knot is easy to tie, and it won't slip.

To tie the surgeon's loop knot, bend the line back to double it. Then tie a simple overhand knot. Instead of snugging this knot tight, make

SURGEON'S LOOP

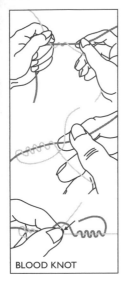

BLOOD KNOT

another wrap in the overhand knot. Now snug the knot tight and clip the tag end.

Blood knot – The blood knot is good for adding new line to old line on your reel.

To tie the blood knot, overlap the two lines 4-5 inches end to end. Wrap one around the other 5 times. Next, wrap the second line around the first line 5 times in the opposite direction. Last, pass both ends back through the center opening in opposite directions. While holding these tag ends, snug the line up tight. Then trim the ends.

Line end knot – This knot is used for tying line to an empty reel spool. It's simple and allows the line to slide down snug against the spool.

Begin by looping the line around the reel spool. Then tie a simple overhand knot around the standing line to form a slip knot. Last, tie another overhand knot in the end of the line to anchor the slip knot when the line is drawn tight. Snug the line tightly around the reel spool and trim the tag end.

Hooks, Sinkers, Floats

Hooks, sinkers and floats are basic components in many fishing rigs. Different combinations of hooks, sinkers and floats produce rigs that can be used on everything from small panfish to large and agressive gamefish. These items of terminal tackle come in many different sizes and designs for a wide variety of applications and purposes.

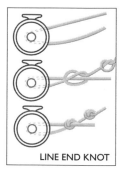

LINE END KNOT

Hooks:
Getting to the Point

Hooks run the gamut from tiny wire hooks for trout to giant forged hooks for such saltwater brutes as sharks and marlin. Hooks also come in different thicknesses, temper (springiness), barb configurations and other features. Different styles of hooks bear different names: Aberdeen, O Shaughnessy, Carlisle, Limerick, etc. With so many variables, it's easy to understand how a beginning angler can feel intimidated when faced with choosing just the right hook. Making good hook selections, however, is easy if you follow a few basic guidelines.

First, buy quality hooks, stick with popular brand names that are most widely advertised and distributed.

Second, pay special attention to hook size. The simple rule is to use small hooks for small fish and big hooks for big fish.

It's important to understand the system manufacturers use to label hook sizes. Smaller hooks are "number-sized," the larger its number, the

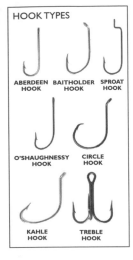

HOOK TYPES

ABERDEEN HOOK — BAITHOLDER HOOK — SPROAT HOOK

O'SHAUGHNESSY HOOK — CIRCLE HOOK

KAHLE HOOK — TREBLE HOOK

smaller the hook. For instance, a #32 hook is tiny and used in small flies. A #10 hook is much larger and might be suitable for bluegill or perch. A #1 hook is larger still and a good size for crappie, walleye, small bass and catfish.

At this point, numbering switches over to the aught system and heads in the other direction. After a #1 hook, the next largest size is a 1/0 (pronounced one-aught), followed by 2/0, 3/0 and so on. These larger hooks are used for bigger bass and catfish, pike, muskies, stripers, lake trout, etc.

Sinkers: A "Weighty" Matter

Sinkers are weights that pull the bait down to the level the angler desires. Sinkers are molded – typically from lead – in many different designs and sizes. The type of sinker you use and how you use it depends on what rig and technique you select for the species you're after. In terms of size, use a sinker heavy enough to do the job, but no heavier than it has to be. In most cases, the lighter the sinker, the less noticeable it will be to the fish.

The most common sinkers are those that clamp directly onto the line. Split shot are small round balls that are pinched onto the line along a slit through

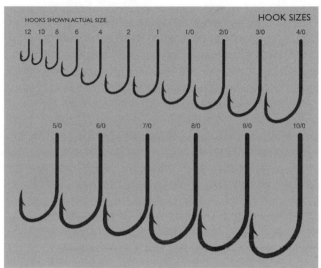

the middle of the sinker. Clincher sinkers are elongated weights that pinch onto the line. Rubbercor sinkers resemble clinchers, but they have a rubber strip through the center. Line is looped behind this rubber to hold the sinker in place.

Sliding sinkers have holes through the middle so the line can slide freely through them. Three common examples are the egg sinker, the bullet sinker and the walking slip sinker. Egg sinkers are used with stationary live bait rigs. The most common use for bullet sinkers is with Texas-rigged plastic worms. Walking slip sinkers are used with slip-sinker rigs to crawl live bait along the bottom.

Various other sinkers are used with bottom-

HOOK SELECTION

BASS: Sizes #2-4/0 forged steel hooks. If using live bait, choose smaller wire hooks. with plastic worms or other artificial lures, use 1/0-4/0 forged steel hooks.

SUNFISH: Sizes #10-#6 light wire hooks. Hooks with a long shank are better and easier to remove when a sunfish swallows the live bait.

CRAPPIE/WHITE BASS: Sizes #4-2/0 light wire hooks.

WALLEYE/SAUGER: Sizes #6-#1 light wire hooks. Some experts prefer baitholder hooks when using minnows, nightcrawlers or leeches.

YELLOW PERCH: #8-#4 light wire hooks.

MUSKELLUNGE/PIKE: Sizes 1/0-6/0 forged steel hooks.

STREAM TROUT: Sizes #10-#1 Aberdeen or baitholder hooks.

STRIPED BASS/HYBRIDS: Sizes 1/0-6/0 forged steel hooks.

LARGE CATFISH: Sizes 1/0-7/0 forged steel hooks. Sizes #8-#1 light wire hooks.

bumping or stationary rigs. Bell swivel sinkers are bell-shaped and have a brass swivel molded in. The line is tied to the swivel, which prevents line twist when you're drift-fishing or bottom-bouncing. Bank sinkers are general purpose bottom sinkers which cast well, slide easily along smooth bottoms and hold well in current. Pyramid and inverted pyramid sinkers have sharp edges and flat sides for gripping in soft, smooth bottoms.

Floats: Visual Strike Indicators

Most fishermen start out as bobber fishermen. They watch a float with a bait suspended beneath it, and they wait for a fish to pull the float under. This is a very simple yet effective and exciting way to fish.

Floats actually serve two purposes. The first is

to suspend the bait at whatever depth the angler wishes, and the second is to signal when a bite is occurring. A float holds the bait as shallow or deep as you desire. It allows you to dangle the bait just above bottom or suspend it over the top of brush, submerged weeds or other underwater cover.

Also, if you want to fish close to the bottom, but you don't know how deep it is, the float can tell you. If your sinker is resting on bottom, there's no weight pulling against the float, so it will lie on its side on the surface. But when you shorten the length of line between your float and sinker so the sinker is no longer touching bottom, the pull will cause the float to ride upright. Then, knowing that your bait is a set distance below your sinker (i.e., 6 inches), you know how deep your bait is and its position relative to the bottom.

Floats come in many materials, shapes and sizes. Most floats are made from hard or foam plastic, wood, cork or porcupine quills. Float designs include round, tubular, barrel-shaped, pear-shaped, quill-shaped, and combinations of these designs.

Long, slender floats are more sensitive to light bites than round ones. Slender floats cast better since there's less wind resistance. I recommend them over round floats for most small-bait, light-tackle situations. If you're fishing for larger fish with larger baits, sensitivity isn't so critical, and round floats will work fine. A good compromise for general use is the combination of a round or barrel float with a quill-like stem passing through the cen-

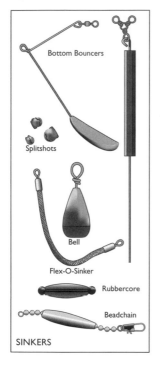

Bottom Bouncers

Splitshots

Bell

Flex-O-Sinker

Rubbercore

Beadchain

SINKERS

ter. The thick part provides buoyancy for the sinker/hook/bait, while the quill adds sensitivity to indicate that you've got a bite.

Most floats attach to the line with a small, spring-loaded wire clip. Others are pegged onto the line and a third group slides up and down the line freely.

Don't make the mistake of fishing with a float that's too large. Select a float that's the smallest possible size considering the weight of your sinker, hook and bait. You want the float to ride high on the surface, but the slightest tug should pull it under. If a float is too large, smaller fish will have trouble swimming down with the bait. This unnatural resistance may alert them to danger. So keep several different-sized floats in your tackle box to match different fishing conditions and rigs.

Snaps, Swivels, Snap Swivels, Split Rings and Leaders

Snaps, swivels, snap swivels, split rings and leaders

are additional types of terminal tackle for use with various rigs and lures.

A snap is a small wire bracket with a safety-pin catch. It's simply a device for changing lures or hooks faster and easier. Tie the line to one end and snap the lure on the other end. To change lures, simply unsnap the catch, take the old lure off, put the new one on and fasten the catch back. A snap, however, adds more weight, drag and hardware that the fish might see. Also, snaps occasionally bend or break under pressure.

A swivel is a small revolving metal link that's often tied between the main line and other components of the terminal rig. A swivel prevents line twist caused by rotating lures or natural baits. Like snaps, swivels also have drawbacks. The best swivels are ball-bearing swivels that revolve under less pressure than other swivels.

The three-way swivel is an important specialty swivel. As its name describes, it has three tie-on rings and is used in some bottom-fishing rigs.

A snap swivel is a combination of a snap and a swivel. Many fishermen use snap swivels with all types of rigs and lures. In most cases, however, they're unnecessary and even ill-advised. Snap swivels add weight, which can deaden the action of a lure. They can create a

SNAPS

SPLIT RING

THREE-WAY SWIVELS

SWIVELS

weak link between line and hook and increase the chance of fouling on brush or weeds.

The split ring is a small overlapping wire ring threaded into the eye of a lure – the line is tied to the ring. This allows the lure more freedom of movement and more lifelike action.

A leader is a length of fishing line or thin wire tied or fastened between the main line and the hook/lure. Leaders serve either of two main purposes: they increase line strength next to the hook and provide a low-visibility connection. This keeps visible line from scaring fish and makes the bait look more natural.

Leaders can also mean an additional length of line tied into a terminal rig to add extra hooks.

Rigs for Everyday Fishing

Following are explanations and diagrams of nine basic rigs, including how to tie them and where and how to use them. Sizes of hooks, sinkers, floats and lines in these rigs will vary from one fishing situation to the next, depending on size and strength of target fish, water depth, bottom type, amount of current and other variables.

Fixed-Bobber Rig

This is the old standby float/sinker/hook rig that catches almost anything. It's used mainly in calm water (ponds, lakes, rivers or pools of streams). It works with both poles and casting tackle, although it's awkward to cast with more than 3 feet of line between the bobber and hook.

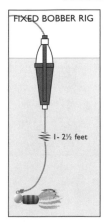

FIXED BOBBER RIG

1- 2½ feet

To assemble this rig, first tie the hook to the end of the line. Next, fasten a split shot, clincher or Rubbercor sinker 6 inches up the line. Clamp or wrap the sinker tightly onto the line so it won't slip down. Last, attach a bobber onto the line at the desired distance above the sinker. The bobber can be adjusted up or down the line to float the bait at whatever depth you desire.

Always balance the size of the sinker and float. Use just enough sinker to take the bait down, then match this with a float barely large enough to hang on the surface. When a fish is nibbling, the bobber will twitch on the surface. When the fish takes the bait, the bobber will move away fast or be yanked underwater. That's the time to set the hook!

Slip-Bobber Rig

The slip-bobber rig is so-named because the bobber slides freely up and down the line. It allows you to offer the bait at any desired length.

The slip-bobber rig is similar to the fixed-bobber rig, with the exception of the free-sliding bobber. Pass the line through the middle of the bobber and run it up the line first. Next, attach a sinker 6 inches up the line. The bobber will slide down and rest atop the sinker. Then tie the

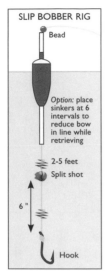

SLIP BOBBER RIG

Bead

Option: place sinkers at 6 intervals to reduce bow in line while retrieving

2-5 feet
Split shot

6 "

Hook

hook on the end of the line. Last, a bobber stop is attached to the line above the bobber that gives the depth where you want to fish. For instance, to fish 5 feet deep, tie the bobber stop 5 feet up the line from the hook.

A bobber stop is a short piece of plastic tube with thread tied loosely around it. To use this stop, run it up the line first, then follow with the float, sinker and hook as described above.

When casting with a slip-bobber rig, the bobber, sinker, hook and bait are near the end of the line. When the rig hits the water, the weight of the sinker and hook pulls the line through the bobber until it hits the stop.

Bottom Rig

This is the basic rig for fishing on the bottom without a float. Bottom rigs are used for bottom-feeding species. This rig is built around a three-way swivel. Tie the main line into one ring of the swivel. Tie a 12-inch leader on the second ring of the swivel, and tie a bank or bell swivel sinker on the other end of this leader. Last, tie an 18-inch leader into the third ring of the swivel. The hook and bait go on the end of this leader.

BOTTOM RIG

The bottom rig is highly versatile. It can be used from shore or boat, with light or heavy tackle. Length of the leaders for the sinker and hook/bait may be altered as desired. Typically, though, the hook leader should be longer than the sinker leader.

Live-Bait Rig

This stationary rig allows nat-ural action from live bait. It can be used in any type of water

LIVE BAIT RIG

and for a wide variety of fish. To tie this rig, run a sliding egg sinker up the line. Clamp on a BB-size split shot sinker below the sinker, 18 inches up from the end of the line. This split shot keeps the egg sinker from riding down on the bait. Last, tie the hook on the end of the line, and bait it with a min-now or night crawler. The bait can swim freely off the bottom and pull the line through the sinker.

Slip-Sinker Rig

Also called the walking-sinker rig, this rig is used to pull live bait across the bottom, either by troll-ing or casting and slowly cranking in line. This rig is highly effective on walleye, but it can also be used for many other species.

Slide a walking-type sinker up the line, then tie on a small barrel swivel. Tie a 3-foot monofilament leader onto the other end of the barrel swivel, and add the hook at the end of this leader. Bait with a night crawler, leech, crawfish or minnow. Most experts troll or drag slip-sinker rigs with spinning

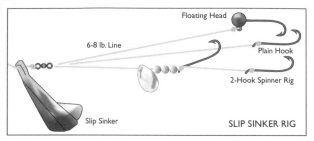

Floating Head

6-8 lb. Line

Plain Hook

2-Hook Spinner Rig

Slip Sinker

SLIP SINKER RIG

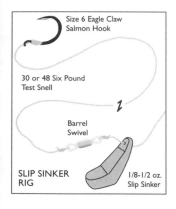

Size 6 Eagle Claw
Salmon Hook

30 or 48 Six Pound
Test Snell

Barrel
Swivel

SLIP SINKER
RIG

1/8-1/2 oz.
Slip Sinker

tackle. When a fish takes the bait, they trip the bail and the fish can run. When the run stops, they reel in slack line until they feel pressure on the line, then they set the hook!

Bottom-Bouncing Rig

Bottom bouncers are weighted wire devices used to troll baits along snaggy bottoms. Thin steel wire is bent into an "L" shape. A lead weight is molded around the center of the long arm. The short arm has a ring for tying on a 3-foot leader and hook. The main line is tied into the 90-degree bend of the "L" between the two arms.

The bottom bouncer is mainly used from a boat. It is lowered to the bottom and

3-4 feet

Bait doctor   Rapala

BOTTOM BOUNCING

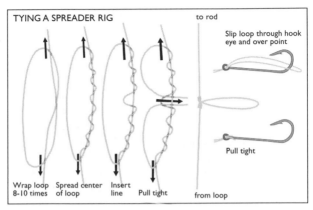

TYING A SPREADER RIG

to rod

Slip loop through hook eye and over point

Pull tight

from loop

Wrap loop 8-10 times
Spread center of loop
Insert line
Pull tight

pulled slowly through likely structure. Enough line should be let out so the bottom bouncer is trailing well behind the boat. The wire holds the weight up off the bottom and the leader and baited hook float behind, just above the bottom.

Two-Hook Panfish Rig

This is a deep-water rig and is fished "tightline" fashion (no float) from a boat. The sinker is on the bottom of this rig, and it's jigged slowly off bottom while two baited hooks dangle above it.

First, tie a bell swivel sinker to the end of the line. Next, tie a surgeon's knot 18 inches above the swivel to form a loop that is big enough to stretch 3 inches. Now tie an identical loop 18 inches up from this first loop. Last, add hooks to the loops in the following manner. Pinch the loop closely together so the line is doubled, then run it through the eye of a thin wire hook (#2-1/0). Then open the loop and pull the hook back through it. Slide the hook tight at the end of the loop, and add bait.

Texas-Rigged Plastic Worm

The Texas-rigged worm is the favorite way to use plastic worms. A Texas-rigged worm is weedless and can be crawled through thick cover.

Start by running a sliding bullet sinker up the line ($^1/_8$ - $^3/_8$ oz. for depths up to 10 feet), then tie on a plastic worm hook. Insert the point of the hook $^1/_2$ inch into the head of the worm. Now pull the point out the side of the worm, and slide the worm up the shank of the hook until the eye is pulled into the head of the worm. Last, rotate the hook and reinsert the point into the side of the worm, completely covering the barb. Done correctly, the worm will hang straight with the hook in place.

Rigged in this manner, the sinker will slide freely along the line. Many anglers prefer to peg the sinker at the head of the worm. This can be done by

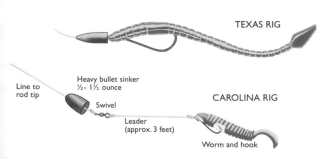

TEXAS RIG

Line to rod tip

Heavy bullet sinker $^1/_2$ - 1$^1/_2$ ounce

Swivel

CAROLINA RIG

Leader (approx. 3 feet)

Worm and hook

using a screw-in sinker or by inserting the small point of a flat toothpick to provide resistance. Then slide the sinker down the line to the head of the worm, and it'll stay in place.

Carolina-Rigged Plastic Worm

Where the Texas-rigged worm is meant for fishing in heavy cover, the Carolina-rigged worm is designed for open structure fishing and covering long distances of a submerged channel dropoff, sunken point, bank, etc. It's very similar to the live-bait rig, except it uses a plastic worm for bait. It's also a very easy rig to use. You simply make a long cast, allow the rig to sink to the bottom, then crank it back in very slowly. There are two basic presentations: dragging – pulling sideways with the rod tip; and small hops by making vertical lifts with the rod tip.

To make a Carolina rig, run a heavy bullet slip sinker(½-1 oz.) up the line; then tie a barrel swivel on the end of the line. Next, tie a 3-foot leader with a hook and plastic worm or lizard on the end. With this rig, the bait is usually fished with the point exposed. Do this by inserting the point of the hook into the head of the worm/lizard and then threading the worm around the bend of the hook and up the shaft. Last, pull the point out the top of the bait, and pull the bait up to straighten it. The worm/lizard should hang straight on the hook.

6. NATURAL BAIT AND ARTIFICIAL LURES

There are two broad categories of baits: natural and artificial.

Natural baits are organic. They include minnows, worms, insects, crawfish, leeches, frogs, cut bait (fish pieces) – a wide variety of living or once-living critters.

Artificial baits include a vast range of lures. Some mimic natural bait. Others bear no resemblance to any natural food, yet they have some attraction that causes fish to bite. (Besides being hungry, fish strike artificial lures because they're mad, greedy, curious or impulsive.)

The list of categories of artificial baits includes top-waters, spinners, crankbaits, soft plastics, jigs, spoons and flies. Further, these categories can be broken down into individual types of baits. For example, soft plastics include plastic worms, lizards, grubs, crawfish, tubes, eels, minnows and more.

So, which should you use: natural bait or artificials? Anglers have faced this decision since the first artificial lures were invented. (Before this, natural baits were the only choice.) Basically, this is a matter of personal preference, convenience and bait capabilities. Each has certain advantages over the other.

Fish usually prefer natural bait over artificials. A bluegill will eat a real earthworm before it will a plastic one. If a live crawfish is retrieved next to an artificial crawfish, a bass will recognize and take the live one. These are examples of why more fish caught in North America are taken on natural bait. It's hard to beat Mother Nature.

So why even bother with artificial baits? There are several reasons. First, many anglers enjoy the challenge of using artificials. Since fish are harder to catch on artificials, these anglers feel there's more reward in fooling the fish with them. These people are fishing more for sport than for meat.

Second, artificial baits are more convenient. You don't have to dig or trap them, and you don't have to keep them alive and fresh. Most can be kept in a tackle box indefinitely and fished with no advance preparation.

Third, artificial lures have certain capabilities and attractions that natural baits don't have. While natural baits are normally used with a stationary or slow-moving presentation, artificials may be retrieved fast to cover a lot of water quickly. They sometimes cause inactive fish to strike out of impulse or anger as the bait runs by (the "catch-it-before-it-gets-away" syndrome). On the other hand, this same fish might ignore a minnow hanging under a bobber.

So, when deciding which to use, weigh the advantages of natural bait versus artificials as they relate to your particular fishing situation. Which is more important: making a good catch, or enjoying a sporty challenge? How difficult is it to get and keep natural bait? Which type bait is more likely to suit your fish's mood and location and the technique you'll use to try for it?

Using Natural Bait

To use natural bait, you have to get it, keep it fresh, hook it on properly, and offer it with the right presentation. Following are guidelines for fishing with several popular natural baits.

But first, although the following outlines tell you how to catch your own bait, in many cases it's more practical to buy bait from a bait/tackle dealer. True, catching bait can be almost as much fun as catching fish, but I usually buy my bait to save as much time as possible for fooling the fish.

One other note: fish normally prefer fresh, active bait to old, lifeless bait. This is why I always keep fresh bait on my hook. If my minnow quits swimming, I replace it with a new one!

Worms – Worms are the most popular natural bait. They include large night crawlers and a variety of smaller earthworms. Worms can be used to catch a variety of panfish and sportfish.

2-HOOK NIGHT CRAWLER HARNESS

AIR-INJECTED NIGHT CRAWLER

#4, #6 or #8 hook

air injector

Worms are easy to collect. You can dig for them in moist, rich soil in gardens, around barnyards and under rotting leaves or logs. Night crawlers can be collected on a grassy lawn at night following a warm rain. Place worms in a small container partially filled with loose crumbled dirt. Make sure any top has holes so the worms can breathe.

Keep the worm can or box out of the sun so the worms won't overheat and die. Many anglers keep their worms in a cooler.

There are several methods for using worms. With a stationary rig (bobber rig, bottom rig), gob one or more worms onto the hook, running the point through the middle of the worm's body several times with the ends dangling free. When fishing for small panfish, don't put too much worm on the hook, since these fish have small mouths. But when fishing for large fish, the more worms on the hook, the better.

If you're fishing for walleye or bass with a walking slip-sinker or a bottom bouncer, hook the

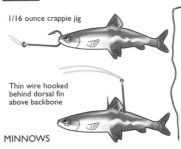

1/16 ounce crappie jig

Thin wire hooked
behind dorsal fin
above backbone

MINNOWS

worm once through
the head so the body
can trail out behind.
When drift-fishing in a
stream for trout, hook
the worm through the
middle of the body
and allow the two
ends to dangle.

Minnows – Shiners, tuffies (fatheads) and gold-fish are popular minnow species that are sold in bait stores. Also, other small minnows can be caught from ponds, streams and lakes. Anglers routinely use minnows to catch crappie, bass, walleye, catfish, stripers and other fish.

One of the easiest ways to catch minnows is to set a wire basket trap. Bait the trap with a piece of bread and drop it into a pond or creek where minnows live. Leave it for a few hours, then retrieve it with its catch inside. Minnows may also be seined or caught with a cast net. However, seines and nets are expensive, and both take a fair amount of know-how to use. For these reasons, I don't recommend them for beginning fishermen.

Minnows must be cared for properly, or they will die quickly. Keep their water cool and fresh. I use Styrofoam buckets instead of metal or plastic, because Styrofoam keeps the water cooler. I never put more than four dozen minnows in a bucket to avoid overcrowding. If the water in a bucket becomes too warm or stale, the minnows will rise to the surface, and you must take quick action to save them. Exchange the old water for fresh. On extremely hot days, add chunks of ice to keep the water cool. Store minnows in the refrigerator and change their water as often as needed.

When I fish with minnows, I put them on the hook two ways. If I'm using a stationary rig, I hook the minnow through the back under the main fin. This allows it to swim naturally. But if I'm using a moving rig like a bottom-bouncer, walking slip sinker or two-hook rig, I hook the minnow through both lips, from bottom to top.

Crickets/Grasshoppers – You can catch grasshoppers in grassy or weedy fields either by hand or with a butterfly net. To catch crickets, look under rocks, planks or logs, and catch them by hand or net.

Place grasshoppers or crickets in a cricket box, or make your own container by punching holes in a coffee can that has a plastic lid. Cut a small round hole in the lid, and keep it covered with masking tape. Peel the tape back to deposit grasshoppers or crickets as you catch them. When you want to get one out, peel the tape back, shake an insect out of the hole, then stick the tape back over the hole.

Grasshoppers and crickets should be stored in a cool, shady place. Each day add a damp paper towel for moisture and a table-

CRICKET

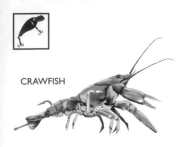

CRAWFISH

spoon of corn meal for food.

Grasshoppers and crickets are normally used with bobber rigs or bottom rigs. They are hooked by inserting the point behind the tail and running it the length of the body and out at the head.

Crawfish – Crawfish are found in most freshwater lakes and streams. Many anglers think of them as good bass baits, but they are also deadly on catfish. Pieces of crawfish tail are irresistible to sunfish.

The best way to gather crawfish is by wading in a shallow stream and slowly turning over flat rocks. When you see a crawfish, ease a tin can (with holes punched in the bottom) up behind it, and then poke at its head with a stick. Crawfish swim backward to escape, so it should back up into the can. When the crawfish goes in, lift the can quickly.

Keep crawfish in a Styrofoam minnow bucket half-filled with water. They can be kept several days if refrigerated.

When handling crawfish, be careful to avoid their pinchers, which can cause painful injury. Hold them by the body just behind the pinchers.

Live crawfish should be hooked in the back section of the tail, from the bottom through the top. They are usually fished on or near bottom with a standard bottom rig or live-bait rig. They can also be trolled slowly along bottom with a slip-sinker rig or bottom bouncer. And once in awhile, they should be fished just above bottom with a bobber rig.

Leeches – Several kinds of leeches inhabit North American waters, but only ribbon leeches are widely used for bait. These leeches squirm actively when held; less desirable leeches are lifeless when held.

To trap leeches, put dead minnows, liver, beef kidney or bones into a large coffee can and mash the top of the can almost shut. Sink the can in leech-infested waters overnight, and rapidly pull the can up the next morning. Leeches keep well in water-filled minnow buckets placed in the shade.

Leeches work well suspended under a bobber, since they squirm continuously. They may be trolled or crawled across bottom on a live-bait rig, slip-sinker rig or bottom-bouncer rig. They are also frequently used as a trailer on a leadhead jig. To hook a leech, run the point of the hook through the head.

Cut Bait – Pieces or entrails of baitfish are excellent for catching catfish. Larger shad, herring, smelt and other oily baitfish are best. These can be netted, cut into square inch chunks and hooked onto bottom rigs. Also, a small slice of panfish meat adds to the attraction of a small jig for sunfish, white bass, crappie and yellow perch.

Using Artificial Baits

Live worms and leeches wiggle on the hook. Live minnows swim. Live crawfish scoot across rocks or mud. But artificial baits hang motionless in the water until the angler gives them life by casting and retrieving. In most cases, the more skillfully this is done, the more fish a user will catch. This is why many anglers consider artificial baits more challenging than natural baits. You've got to add the life!

Following are short descriptions of various artificial lures and how to use them.

Topwaters – This is the oldest category of artificial baits and one of the best. Bass, muskies, pike, stripers, white bass, trout and other species feed on the surface, normally in warm months and low-light periods of early morning, late afternoon and night. Sometimes, though, fish will hit topwaters in the middle of a bright day. Basically, if you see surface-feeding activity, give topwaters a try.

Topwater baits include wood and plastic lures in a broad variety of shapes and actions.

Poppers (also called chuggers) have scooped-out heads which make slapping sounds when pulled with short, quick jerks.

Floating minnows rest motion-

BASS PRO SHOPS
XPSLOCUST

BERKLEY FRENZY
WALKER

EXCAL-ULTRALIGHT
GST MINNOW

ARBOGAST HULA
POPPER

ARBOGAST JITTERBUG

STRIKE KING ELITE
BUZZBAIT

less and then swim with a quiet, subtle side-to-side action when reeled in.

Stickbaits resemble cigars with hooks attached. They dart across the surface in a zig-zag pattern when pulled with short, quick snaps of the rod tip.

Crawlers have concave metal lips. This bait wobbles back and forth and makes a popping noise on a steady retrieve.

Buzz baits have revolving metal or plastic blades that boil the water on a steady retrieve.

If fish are actively feeding on the surface, use a lure that works fast and makes a lot of noise. But if fish aren't active, select a quieter lure and work it slowly. (In this case, after the lure hits the water, let it sit still until all ripples disappear. Then twitch the lure slightly, and hold on!)

When casting a topwater lure, be ready for a strike when it hits the water. Sometimes fish see it coming through the air and take it immediately.

When a fish strikes a topwater lure, wait until the lure disappears underwater before setting the hook. This takes nerves of steel, since the natural tendency is to jerk the instant the strike occurs. However, a short delay will give the fish time to take the lure down and turn away with it, which increases your chance of getting a good hookset.

Spinners – This bait category includes spinnerbaits and in-line spinners.

Spinnerbaits are shaped like an open safety pin. A rotating blade is attached to the upper arm; a leadhead body, skirt and hook are on the lower

ABU GARCIA REFLEX
SPINNER

STRIKE KING COMPACT
SILHOUETTE
SPINNERBAIT

BERKLEY SCENT VENT

arm. This design makes a spinnerbait semi-weedless, so it can be worked through vegetation, brush, timber and stumps with few hang-ups.

Spinnerbaits come in a wide variety of sizes and blade configurations. Some have one blade, while others have two or more. Some have Colorado or Indiana blades (oval-shaped) for slower vibrations with more "thump," while others have willowleaf blades (elongated/ pointed) for faster, higher-pitched vibrations. Colorado/Indiana blades are better for slower retrieves for inactive fish. Willowleaf blades are made to retrieve faster (especially in current) and for fish that are actively chasing baitfish.

Spinnerbaits are normally associated with bass fishing, but they're also good on muskies and pike. Very small spinnerbaits can be effective on small panfish like crappie and sunfish.

The blade on an in-line spinner is attached to the same shaft as the body, and it revolves around it. Because of this compact design, in-line spinners work well in current. These lures are typically used for smallmouth bass, rock bass, trout and other stream species.

Spinners are a good artificial lure for beginning anglers. In most cases, all you have to do is cast them out and reel them in. As your skills increase, you'll learn to vary retrieves and crawl spinnerbaits through cover or across bottom. In any case, when you feel a bump or see your line move sideways, set the hook immediately!

Crankbaits – This is another good lure family for beginners. Crankbaits are so-named because they have built-in actions. All you have to do is cast them and then crank the reel handle. The retrieve causes these baits to wiggle, dive and come to life.

COTTON CORDELL GRAPPLER SHAD

LUHR-JENSEN RADAR 10

STRIKE KING WILD SHINER SUSPENDING JERK BAIT

Crankbaits are used mainly for largemouth and smallmouth bass, white bass, walleye, sauger, muskies and pike. They are effective in reservoirs, lakes and streams, around rocks, timber, docks, bridges, roadbeds and other structure. Generally they're not effective in vegetation, since their treble hooks foul in the weeds. However, crankbaits can be effective when retrieved close to weeds or over the top of submerged vegetation.

BILL LEWIS RAT-L-TRAP BLEEDING SHAD

STRIKE KING BLEEDING BAIT SPINNERBAIT

There are two sub-categories of crankbaits: "floater/divers," and "vibrating." Floater/divers usually have plastic or metal lips. They float on the surface at rest, but when the retrieve starts, they dive underwater and wiggle back and forth. Usually, the larger a bait's lip, the deeper it will run.

One of the secrets to success with floater/divers is to keep them bumping bottom or cover objects. To do this, you must retrieve them so they will dive as deeply as possible. Maximum depth may be achieved by using smaller line (6-12 pound test is perfect), cranking at a medium pace instead of too fast, pointing your rod tip down toward the water during the retrieve and making long casts. Once the bait hits bottom, vary the retrieve speed or try stop-and-go reeling to trigger strikes. Keep it working along bottom as long as possible before it swims back up to the rod tip.

Sometimes a floater/diver crankbait gets "out-of-tune" and won't swim in a straight line. Instead, it veers off to one side or the other. To retune a lure, bend the eye (where you tie the line) in the direction opposite the way the lure is veering. Make small adjustments with a pair of needlenose pliers, and test the lure's track after each adjustment to get it swimming straight.

Vibrating crankbaits are used in relatively shallow water where fish are actively feeding. These are sinking baits, so the retrieve must be started shortly after they hit the water. They should be reeled fast to simulate baitfish fleeing from a predator. This speed and tight wiggling action excites larger fish into striking.

Soft Plastics – This family of baits includes plastic worms, grubs, minnows, tubes, lizards, crawfish, eels and other live bait imitations. These baits are natural-feeling and lifelike to fish. They are used mainly on bass, white bass, stripers, panfish, crappie, walleye and other species.

BERKLEY MICRO POWER FROG

Soft plastics are very versatile lures. They can be fished without weight on the surface, or they can be weighted with a sinker or jighead and fished below the surface. They can be rigged weedless and fished through weeds, brush or stumps.

BERKLEY POWER LEECH

Plastic worms are among the most popular of soft plastic lures. The most common way to use them is to crawl or hop them along bottom structure. To do this, rig the worm according to the instructions under Texas-Rigged Plastic Worms in the previous chapter. Use a small slip sinker for fishing shallow water and a heavier sinker for deeper water. A good rule of thumb is to use a $^1/_8$-oz. slip sinker in depths up to 6 feet, a $^1/_4$-

BERKLEY POWER TUBE

BERKLEY POWER CRAW

BERKLEY POWER LIZARD

BOMBER MODEL 8A

oz. sinker from 6-12 feet, and a $^3/_8$ - $^1/_2$-oz. sinker in water deeper than 12 feet.

Cast the worm toward the structure and allow it to sink to the bottom. (You'll feel it hit or see your line go slack.) Hold your rod tip in the 10 o'clock position and reel up slack. Now quickly lift the rod tip to the 11 o'clock position without reel-

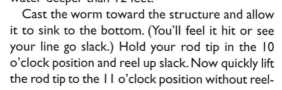

ing. This lifts the worm off the bottom and swims it forward a short distance. Then allow the worm to fall back to the bottom, reel up slack line and repeat the process. This lift/drop/reel sequence should be repeated until the worm exits the main target area (tree top, brush, weedbed, etc.)

When hopping a plastic worm, be alert for any taps or bumps, and always watch your line for sudden, unnatural pulses or sideways movements. Sometimes strikes are obvious and easy to detect. Other times they are light and subtle. If you know you've got a bite, reel up slack line and set the hook immediately. But if you're not sure, reel up slack and hold the bait still for a few seconds. If nothing happens, tug on the bait ever so slightly. If you feel something tug back, set the hook!

To set the hook with a plastic worm, lower your rod tip to the 9 o'clock position, then set hard and fast with your wrists and forearms. If you don't feel that you have a good hookset, set again. This method applies to tackle spooled with line above 10-pound test. When you're using lighter line, set with less force, or you may break your line.

Virtually all soft plastic baits can be fished with the same lift/drop/reel technique described above. Also, grubs can be hopped along bottom or swum through mid-depth areas with a steady retrieve. Lizards and eels can be slithered through weeds and brush. Minnows can be threaded through sunken flats and timber. Crawfish can be bumped through rocks. Weightless worms and plastic stick lures can be worked over sunken vegetation and other cover. Experiment with various baits to see which one the fish prefer.

Jigs – If there's such a thing as a universal bait, the leadhead jig is it. These balls of lead with hooks running out the back can be used in a wide range of circumstances to catch almost all kinds of freshwater fish. Jigs are basic baits and all anglers should learn to use them effectively.

Jigs come in a wide range of sizes. Tiny jigs ($^1/_{32}$-oz.) will take trout or small panfish in shallow water. A 1-oz. jig might be used to bump bottom in heavy current for walleye or sauger. The most popular jig sizes are $^1/_{16}$, $^1/_8$ and $^1/_4$ oz.

Many veteran anglers keep different size jigs in their tackle boxes and then select the right size for a particular fishing situation. This selection is based on the size of the target fish, depth of water and amount of wind and current. The bigger the fish, the deeper the water, and the stronger the wind and current, the heavier the jig should be.

BOMBER FLAIR HAIR JIG

Jigs are almost always "dressed" with an artificial trailer or live bait. Some jigs are made with hair, feather or rubber skirts wrapped around the hook. Others come pre-rigged with plastic grubs. But the majority of jigs are sold without any trailer, leaving this choice up to the angler. You may install your own trailer

STRIKE KING
BLEEDING BITSY BUG JIG

(plastic grub, tube, small worm, pork rind), or you may prefer hooking on a live minnow, night crawler or leech. Also, in addition to trailers, some jigs have small spinners attached to the head of the lure to add flash.

There are several effective jig retrieves. The basic one is the lift/drop: allow the jig to sink to the bottom, then hop it along the bottom with short lifting jerks of the rod tip. (This is similar to the lift/drop/reel method for fishing a plastic worm, except faster.) Another popular retrieve is the steady pull, swimming the jig in open water or just above bottom, sometimes grazing stumps, rocks or other structure.

A third retrieve is vertical jigging. Lower the jig straight down to bottom or into cover, lift it with the rod tip, then allow it to sink back down. Most strikes come when the bait is dropping.

As with plastic worms, strikes on jigs may be very hard or extremely light. An angler using a jig will usually feel a bump or tick as a fish sucks in the bait. The key to detecting this is keeping a tight line at all times. If you feel a bump or see unnatural movement, set the hook immediately. There's no waiting with jigs.

Spoons – Metal spoons are the "old faithfuls" of artificial lures. They've been around a long time, and they're still producing. They are excellent for catching bass, walleye, pike, muskies and white bass.

Some spoons are designed to be fished on the surface, while others are for underwater use.

In both cases, the standard retrieve is a slow, steady pull. Sometimes, however, an erratic stop/go retrieve may trigger more strikes.

JOHNSON SPRITE SPOON

One special use for spoons is for fishing around or through weeds and surface-matted grass. Topwater spoons will ride over the thickest lily pads, moss, etc. Spoons retrieved underwater will flutter and dart through reeds and grass with minimal hang-ups. In this situation, a spoon with a weedguard over a single hook is recommended.

Trailers are frequently added to a spoon's hook for extra attraction. Pork strips or plastic or rubber skirts are standard trailers. When adding a skirt to a spoon's hook, run the hook's point through the skirt from back to front so the skirt will billow out during the retrieve.

Summary

I have described rods, reels and line as "tools" for fishing. Baits are also tools in the truest sense. They are objects designed to help you catch fish. Different baits serve specific purposes. You must learn what various baits are designed to do, then apply them where they work best.

You start to do this by reading, but then you must apply what you read on the water. There's no better teacher than experience. Lakes and streams are your laboratory. This is where you'll carry out your experiments with various fishing tools.

7. FISHING TECHNIQUES

In this chapter, we'll move from general information to specifics. This section will teach you practical, step-by-step techniques for taking fish from a variety of fishing spots that you might encounter.

Obviously it's impossible to cover all techniques for all fish. Instead, we'll look at the best opportunities and simplest techniques. Also, I'll help you identify prime fishing locations in different types of waters, then tell you how to make them pay off.

Where Fish Live

The first step in catching fish is knowing where to find them. On each outing you must first study your water to determine where fish are located.

The concept of structure is the key in determining where fish are holding and where you can catch them. Remember that most fish will tend to gather in predictable places, and these places fall into what anglers call structure.

First, you need to figure out where fish are most likely to be found. Then decide which combination of tackle, bait and method will be most effective in catching them. Review this process each time you fish. First, location. Where should the fish be? Then, presentation. What's the best way to catch them?

How to Fish Ponds and Small Lakes

Farm ponds and small lakes are scattered throughout North America. They are the best and most numerous of all fishing waters.

Some ponds are formed naturally but most ponds and small lakes are manmade to provide water for livestock, irrigate fields and prevent erosion. Others were built strictly for recreation.

Analyzing Ponds and Small Lakes

When you get to a pond or small lake, your fishing starts before you wet a line. First you should study the pond to determine its characteristics. Some ponds have flat basins, while others have a shallow end with ditches running into it and a deep end with a dam. Many ponds have brush, weeds, trees, logs or other structure. Take note of all the combinations of depths and structure to determine which combination is holding the fish.

Again, consider your target species' basic nature. Where that fish will be located will vary according to the time of year and water conditions. For instance, bass might be in the shallows in spring and in deeper water in the summer. However, in the hottest months they might still feed in the shallows during night or at dawn and dusk. These are the types of things you must learn before you can make an educated guess about where to find fish.

Techniques for Fishing Ponds and Small Lakes

Most ponds and small lakes support what biologists call warm water fisheries: sunfish, crappie, bass, catfish and bullheads. Some spring-fed ponds hold trout. Let's take these species one at a time and look specifically at how to catch them.

Sunfish – Bluegill and other sunfish are usually the most plentiful fish in ponds and small lakes, and they always seem willing to bite. In spring, early summer and fall, they stay in shallow to medium-deep water (2-10 feet). In hottest summer and coldest winter, they normally move deeper, though they may still occasionally feed in the shallows.

Small sunfish love to hold around brush, logs, weeds, piers and other cover. On cloudy days or in dingy water, these fish often hang around edges of such structure. This is true during the early morning and late afternoon. But during the part of the day when the sun is brightest, sunfish swim into brush or vegetation, under piers or tight to stumps and logs. On sunny days, they like to hide in shady areas.

If possible, get out early to fish for sunfish. Take a long panfish pole or light-action spinning or spin-cast rod and reel spooled with 4- or 6-pound test line. Tie a fixed-bobber rig with a long-shank wire hook (#6 or #8), a little split shot and a bobber.

Bait with earthworms, crickets or grasshoppers. Thread on a small worm, or use a small piece of nightcrawler. A whole cricket or grasshopper is the best bait for bluegills.

Next, adjust the bobber so your bait hangs midway between the surface and the bottom. If you can't see the bottom and you don't know how deep the pond is, begin fishing 2-4 feet deep. If you don't catch fish, experiment with other depths.

A fallen tree or log can form an ideal hiding place for bass, sunfish and other species. Be sure to carefully scout a small lake or pond for such underwater structure.

If you think sunfish may be holding around weeds close to the bank, drop your bait in next to the weeds. The bobber should float upright. If it's laying on its side, the bait is probably on the bottom. In this case, shorten the distance between the bobber and hook to suspend the bait.

Don't stand right over the spot you're fishing. The fish might see you and become spooky. Wear natural-colored clothing and avoid actions that might scare the fish.

Sunfish will usually bite with little hesitation so if you don't get a bite in a couple of minutes, twitch your bait to get the fish's attention. Keep your bait close to cover, and look for openings where you can drop the bait. If you're not getting bites, try fishing around another type of structure, or try a deeper area.

Remember always to "think structure." Don't drop your bait at some random spot in the middle of the pond. Keep moving until you begin catching fish and work the area slowly and thoroughly.

A special opportunity exists during spring when sunfish are spawning. They fan nests in shallow water (2-5 feet deep) around the banks and in the shallows. The nests are about the size of a dinner

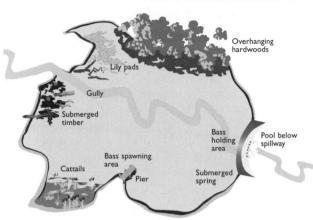

Overhanging
hardwoods

Lily pads

Gully

Submerged
timber

Bass
holding
area

Pool below
spillway

Cattails

Bass spawning
area

Pier

Submerged
spring

plate, and appear light against the dark pond bottom. Usually, many nests will be clustered in the same area. Set your bobber shallow and drop your bait right next to the nests, trying not to spook the fish. You're probably better off casting into the beds rather than sneaking in close with a long pole.

Crappie – Fishing for crappie in ponds and small lakes is similar to fishing for sunfish. The fish stay close to structure and stay on the move. The main difference is the bait. Crappie prefer minnows and readily attack small jigs and spinners.

Long poles are a favorite with crappie fishermen. Many crappie experts quietly scull a small boat from one piece of structure to the next, and use a panfish pole to dangle a float rig with a minnow or jig next to cover. They ease their bait down beside a tree or piece of brush, leave it for a moment, pick it up, set it down on the other side, then move to the next spot. This "hunt-and-peck" method is very effective, particularly in spring when fish will be spawning in shallow cover.

Another good crappie technique is to use a slip-bobber rig with a spinning or spin-cast outfit. Hook a live minnow through the back onto a thin wire hook (#2) or through the lips on a lightweight ($1/16$ or $1/32$ oz.) jig. Then cast this rig next to a weedline, brushpile or log.

If you don't get a bite in 5 minutes, try somewhere else. If you get a bite, don't yank if the bobber is just twitching. Wait for the bobber to start moving or disappear beneath the surface before setting the hook. Crappie have soft mouths, so don't set too hard, or you'll rip out the hook.

If you don't catch fish shallow, try deeper water, especially during hot summer months or on bright, clear days. Adjust your bobber up the line and drop your bait right in front of the dam or off the end of a pier. Try casting into the middle of the pond and see what happens. With this method of fishing, 6-10 feet is not too deep.

To cover a lot of water, cast a $1/16$-oz. jig or a small in-line spinner. After casting, count slowly as the bait sinks. After a few seconds, begin your retrieve. Try different counts (depths). If you get a bite, let the bait sink to the same count next time. You may have found the depth where crappie are holding. This technique is called the "countdown" method of fishing with a sinking bait.

When retrieving the jig, move it at a slow to moderate pace, and alternate between a straight pull and a rising/falling path back through the water. With the spinner, a slow, straight retrieve is best.

Bass – Bass fishing is more complicated than fishing for sunfish or crappie, partly because of all the different types of bass tackle and lures. Bass are still members of the sunfish family, however, and they share certain behavior characteristics with bluegill and crappie. Anywhere you're likely to catch these latter fish, you're apt to find bass.

Most experienced anglers go after pond bass with casting or spinning tackle and artificial lures. Casting allows you to reach targets farther away and also to cover more water. Many artificial lures will catch pond bass, but my three favorites are topwaters, spinnerbaits and plastic worms.

Try topwaters early in the morning, late in the afternoon or at night (during summer). Use topwaters when the sky is overcast, especially when the surface is calm. In warmer months, I prefer poppers and propeller baits that make a lot of noise and attract bass from a distance. In early spring, I like a quieter floating minnow.

Cast topwaters close to weeds, beside logs, along dams or anywhere you think bass might be holding. Cast past a particular object, then work the bait up to where you think the fish are. Allow the bait to rest motionless for several seconds, then twitch it just enough to cause the slightest ripple on the water. This is usually when the strike comes!

If a spot looks good, but you don't get a strike, cast back to it several times. Sometimes when bass are "inactive" (aren't feeding), you have to arouse their curiosity or agitate them into striking.

At times, though, bass just won't strike a surface lure. If you don't get any action on a top-water lure in 15 minutes, switch to a spinner-bait and try the same area. Keep your retrieve steady, and try different speeds (fast, medium, slow). You might try "fluttering" the bait – allowing it to sink momentarily after it runs past a log, treetop or other cover. This can trigger a strike from a bass that's following the lure during a steady retrieve.

Don't be afraid to retrieve a spinnerbait through brush and weeds. If you keep reeling while it's coming through cover, this lure is virtually weedless.

Plastic worms are what I call "last resort baits."

Big bass and catfish will sometimes lurk in hollows in a pond or river bank formed by erosion beneath fallen trees. Catfish favor these holes during spawning season.

Bass can be coaxed into striking worms when they won't hit other lures, and plastic worms can be worked slower through thick cover. Plastic worms are good for bass in deep water and are top prospects for mid-day fishing in hot weather.

For pond bass, use a 4-7½ inch plastic worm rigged Texas-style with a ¹/₁₆-¼ oz. sliding sinker. Cast it right into cover or close to it. (Make sure the point of the hook is embedded inside the worm.) Then crawl it slowly through the cover, lifting it with the rod tip, then allowing it to settle back to the bottom.

When fishing lily pads, brush or other thick vegetation, cast to openings and pockets. Cast off points, ends of weedbeds and corners of piers.

If you don't get action in the shallows, and suspect the bass are deeper – change tactics. Locate structure by interpreting what you can from the surface. Find a gully feeding into the shallow end of the pond. Then imagine how the gully runs along the pond bottom, and cast your plastic worm along it.

A second deep-water strategy is to cast a plastic worm into the deep end or along the dam, then crawl it back up the bank. In all cases, however, it's very important to allow your plastic worm to sink to the bottom before starting your retrieve. When casting to deep spots, if you catch a fish, cast back to the same spot. Bass often school in deep water.

There are other baits you might use in special situations. Many ponds have heavy weedbeds or lily pads. You can fish them with a topwater spoon that wobbles over plants and attracts bass lying underneath. Leadhead jigs tipped with a plastic trailer (grub, crawfish, etc.) can be hopped across bottom when searching deep-water areas. Diving crankbaits are good for random casting into deep spots.

Catfish and Bullheads – Catfish and bullheads spend the most time on or near the bottom of small ponds and lakes. While they prefer deep water, however, they may move up and feed in the shallows from time to time. In either location, fish directly on bottom without a float or just above bottom with a float.

Fishing for catfish and bullheads calls for a pick-one-spot-and-wait method. Cats find their food mostly by smell and you have to leave your bait in one place long enough for the scent to spread and for the fish to home in on it.

It's possible to fish for these species with long poles, but I prefer spin-cast or spinning outfits so I can fish farther off the bank. I take at least two rods. I pick a spot on the bank close to deep water. Then I cut a forked stick for each rod and push it into the ground next to the pond's edge. I cast out my lines, prop my rods in the forked sticks, and wait for something to happen.

When using two rods, I tie a bottom rig on one and a slip-bobber rig on the other. This gives the catfish or bullheads a choice of a bait laying on bottom or hanging just above.

Catfish grow much larger than bullheads, so

if catfish are your main target, you need larger hooks. I recommend a #1 or 1/0 sproat or bait-holder hook. If you're fishing for bullheads, select a smaller #6 hook. If you're trying for both species, use something in between — a #2 or #4.

Catfish and bullheads will eat the same baits. Earthworms or nightcrawlers are two favorites. Chicken liver, live or dead minnows, grasshoppers and a wide variety of commercially-made baits also work well. With all these baits, load your hooks. The more bait on them, the more scent you have in the water, and the more likely you are to attract fish.

Cast your baited lines into deep water. With the bottom rig, wait until the sinker is on bottom, then gently reel in line until all the slack is out. With a slip-bobber rig, set the bobber so the bait is suspended just above bottom.

When a fish takes the bottom-rig bait, the rod tip will jump. When there's a bite on the slip-bobber bait, the bobber will dance nervously on the surface. If you get a bite, don't set the hook until the fish starts swimming away. Pick up the rod and get ready to set the hook, but don't exert any pull until the line starts moving steadily off or the bobber goes under and stays. Then strike back hard and begin playing your fish.

If you're not getting bites, stay in one place as long as you can stand it. At a minimum, you should fish in one spot at least 20 minutes before moving somewhere else.

How to Fish Large Lakes and Reservoirs

Large lakes and reservoirs are some of the most popular and accessible fishing locations. Most are public waters with boat ramps, piers and other facilities to accommodate fishermen and usually have large, diverse fish populations.

Natural lakes are plentiful in the northern United States and Canada, in Florida, along major river systems (oxbows) and in the Western mountains. Some have rounded, shallow basins with soft bottoms while others are deep with irregular shapes and bottoms that include reefs, islands and other structure. In many natural lakes, vegetation grows abundantly in shallow areas.

Reservoirs are impoundments formed by damming a river and backing up the floodwaters. In most

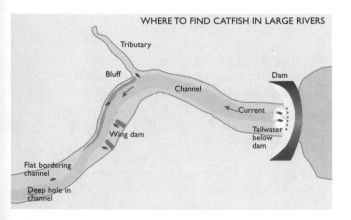

WHERE TO FIND CATFISH IN LARGE RIVERS

Tributary

Bluff

Channel

Dam

Current

Tailwater below dam

Wing dam

Flat bordering channel

Deep hole in channel

cases, the bottoms of reservoirs were once farm-land or forest and water covers old fields, wood-lands, creeks, roads and other features that, when submerged, became structure.

There are two categories of reservoirs: upland and lowland (or mainstream). Upland reservoirs are built in highlands or canyons. They are typically deep and wind through steep terrain. Their coves and creek arms are irregular in shape.

In contrast, lowland reservoirs course through broad, flat valleys. They are wider and shallower than upland reservoirs and typically have a long, trunk with numerous smaller tributary bays.

Analyzing Large Lakes and Reservoirs

You can't fish an entire large lake or reservoir. So choose one small part of it and use the same tactics as you would in ponds or small lakes. Fish react the same to similar conditions in their envi-ronment and the same tactics work in large waters and small. Since they aren't confined, however, fish migrate from one area to another depending on the season, food supply and other factors.

How do you pick the right small part of a big lake? Ask a local tackle store owner where the fish are biting. Watch where other anglers are fishing. Find out if the fish are shallow or deep. Learn the depth where they're biting. Use your information to form an overall picture then key in on a location.

All anglers should learn to use a topographic

map. A "topo" map shows water depth and contour changes on the lake bottom. You can use it to find drop-offs, reefs, flats, creek channels and other types of structure. You can use the map to find these areas where fish are likely to hang out.

Techniques for Fishing Large Lakes and Reservoirs

Again, large lakes and reservoirs support many different fish species. Some have only warm-water fish, some only cold-water fish, and others a mix of the two. When you go fishing, single out which species you'd like to catch, then tailor your efforts to it.

Sunfish — In spring, sunfish migrate into shallow areas to spawn, so look for them in bays and pockets along wind-protected shorelines. Before spawning, sunfish hold around brush, stumps, weeds, rocks or other structure in 2-8 feet of water. Then, as the water temperature climbs into the mid-60° F range, sunfish will move up into 1-4 feet of water and spawn in areas that have firm bottoms.

Long poles or light-action spinning or spin-cast tackle will take these fish. Use fixed or slip-bobber rigs with wiggler worms, crickets or a small hair jig tipped with a maggot for bait. Around cover, keep your bait close in. When fishing a spawning area, drop the bait right into the beds. (In a visible spawning bed, try the outer edge first, then work your way to the center. This keeps fish that are hooked and struggling from spooking other fish.)

After spawning, sunfish head back to deeper water. Many fish will still hold around visible cover, but they prefer to be near deep water. Two classic examples are a weedline on the edge of a drop-off and a steep rocky bank.

Besides a bobber rig, another good way to take sunfish is "jump-jigging." This involves casting a $1/16$-oz. tube jig around weeds or rocks. Use a very light spinning outfit. Slowly reel the tube jig away from the cover and let the jig sink along the edge. Set the hook when you feel a bump or tug. This technique requires a boat, since you have to be over deep, open water casting into the weeds.

Docks, piers and bridges are good places to catch post-spawn sunfish. Usually the fish will be up near the surface, holding under or close to structures. Don't cast far out into the water. The fish are likely to be under your feet! Set your bobber so your bait hangs deeper than you can see, then keep your bait close to the structure.

Crappie – These fish follow the same seasonal patterns as sunfish, except slightly earlier. When spring breaks, crappie head into bays and quiet coves to get ready to spawn. When the water warms into the low-60°F range, they fan out into the shallows. They spawn in or around brush, reeds, stumps, logs, roots, submerged timber, artificial fish attractors or other cover. Crappie spawning depth depends on water color. In dingy water, they may spawn only a foot or two deep. But in clear water, they'll spawn deeper, as far down as 12 feet. A good depth to try is 1 to 2 feet below the depth at which your bait sinks out of sight.

Minnows or small plastic jigs are good baits. Drop them next to or into potential spawning cover. Lower the bait, wait 30 seconds, then move the bait to another spot. When fishing a brush pile or reed patch, try moving the bait around in the cover.

After crappie spawn, they head back toward deeper water and collect along underwater ledges, creek channel banks and other sharp bottom contour breaks. Locate these areas and look for brush, logs or other visible cover. Fish these spots with minnows or jigs. Or, if there is no visible cover, cast jigs randomly from shore. Wait until the jig sinks to the bottom before starting your retrieve. Then use a slow, steady retrieve to work the bait back up the bank. Set the hook when you feel any slight "thump" or when your line twitches.

Fall may be the second best time to catch crappie in large lakes and reservoirs. When the water starts cooling, they move back into shallow areas, holding around cover. Troll slowly through bays, casting jigs or dropping minnows into likely spots.

Bass – Spring, early summer and fall are the three best times for beginning anglers to try for bass. This is when the fish are aggressive and shallow. During these seasons, bass spend most of their time in or near cover like brush, weeds, lily pads, logs, docks, stumps, rocks, riprap and bridge pilings.

In spring, bass spawn in shallow, wind-sheltered coves and shorelines, especially the ones with hard bottoms of sand, gravel or clay. During the spawning season, try topwater minnows, spinnerbaits and plastic lizards in these areas. Bass love to locate their nests next to features that offer protection from egg-eating sunfish.

After spawning, bass may stay shallow for several weeks. This is a good time to fish points – ridges of land that run off into the water. Stand on the tip of a point and fan-cast crankbaits, plastic worms or splashy topwater lures (poppers, prop baits) around the point. Pay special attention to any structure – brush, stumps, rocks or weeds. If you don't get a strike the first time, cast back to it. Sometimes you have to goad bass into striking.

Despite warm water temperatures in summer, good bass fishing can still be found. Try fishing early and late in the day. Some bass will feed in the shallows during these low-light periods, then retreat to deeper water during mid-day. Others will hold along deeper areas or on the edges of shallow flats bordering deeper water. Work your way along reefs, weedlines, channel drop-offs, sunken roadbeds or around boat docks. Also, cast to any isolated cover, such as a log or rock pile.

Crankbaits and spinnerbaits are good lures for hot-weather bass, since you can fish them fast and cover a lot of water. If you go through a likely area without getting a bite, work back through it with a Texas-rigged plastic worm. Move around and try to find where fish are concentrated. In the warm months, this will typically be where a food supply, usually minnows, is available.

In fall, concentrate on shorelines and shallows in coves. Water temperature cools off in these areas first, and this cool-down draws in both baitfish and bass. Use the same tactics and baits you did in spring. Pay special attention to cover spots and the presence of minnows. If you see schools of minnows and bigger fish working around them, cast these areas with a lipless crankbait in shad color.

Catfish/Bullheads – Big lakes can hold big catfish, and the best time to catch them is in late spring during the spawn. These fish move to the banks and look for holes and protected areas to lay their eggs.

Look for banks with big rock bluffs, riprap, etc. Fish around these areas with fixed or slip-bobber rigs baited with gobs of wiggler worms or night crawlers. Set your float so the bait hangs just above the rocks. Use medium strength line (10-20 pound test) and a steel hook (#1-3/0), since the possibility of hooking a big fish is good.

After they spawn, catfish head back to deep-water flats and channels. Normally they spend daylight hours deep, and move up at night to feed in nearby shallows. Find a point or other spot where the bank slopes off into deep water, and fish here from late afternoon well into the night. Use a bottom rig, baited with worms, cut bait, liver, commercial stink bait, or other popular catfish baits.

Walleye – are traditionally deep-water, bottom-hugging fish, but they will frequently feed in the shallows. The determining factor seems to be light penetration into the water. Walleye don't like bright sunlight. But on overcast days, at night, when shallow areas are dingy, or when heavy weed growth provides shade, they may hold and feed in water no deeper than a couple of feet.

Walleye may be the ultimate structure fish. In deep areas, they hold along underwater humps, reefs and drop-offs on hard, clean bottoms, especially those with rock or sand. They prefer water with good circulation and rarely concentrate in dead-water areas like sheltered bays or coves.

Walleye spawn when water temperature climbs into the mid-40°F range. Look for shallows or shoal areas with gravel or rock bottoms that are exposed to the wind. Sloping points, reefs and rock piles close to shore are high-percentage spots. Fish them during low-light periods.

Try a slip-bobber rig baited with a night crawler, leech or live minnow in these areas. Adjust the bobber so the bait is suspended just above bottom. Try casting shallow areas with jigs tipped with live minnows or shallow-running crankbaits.

In early summer, walleye can be caught along weedlines and mid-lake structure, both requiring a boat to properly fish them. When fishing weeds, cast a small jig ($1/16$ or $1/8$ oz.) tipped with a minnow right into the edge of the weeds, then swim it back out. Work slowly along the weedline. Pay special attention to sharp bends in the weedline or areas where the weeds thin out.

Fishing deep structure can be a needle in a haystack situation, so it's best to stay on the move until you locate fish. A bite will feel like a light tap or bump. Release line immediately and allow the fish to swim with the bait. After about 20 seconds, reel up slack, feel for the fish and set the hook.

There are other good methods. Bottom-bouncing rigs trailing night crawlers or minnows can be productive along deep structure or submerged points. This is the same principle as using the slip-sinker rig. Drop your line to the bottom, engage the reel, then drag the rig behind you as you drift or troll. A slip-bobber rig drifted across this structure is also a good bet.

Northern Pike – Pike fishing is best in spring, early summer and fall, when these fish are in quiet, weedy waters. Look for pike in bays, sloughs, flats and coves with submerged weedbeds, logs or other structure. Pike like fairly shallow water – 3-10 feet.

Pike can get big, and even small ones are tough fighters, so use fairly heavy tackle. (Use 12-20 pound line.) Their sharp teeth can easily cut monofilament, so always rig with a short steel leader ahead of your lure or bait.

Find access to likely cover and cast a large, brightly-colored spoon next to or over it. If you have a boat, motor to the upwind side of a shallow bay and drift slowly downwind, casting to clumps of weeds and weed edges. Retrieve the spoon steadily, but if pike don't seem interested, pump the spoon up and down or jerk it erratically to get their attention. Other good lures for pike are large spinnerbaits, in-line spinners, large floating minnows and wide-wobbling crankbaits.

Live-bait fishing is extremely effective. Use a large minnow suspended under a fixed-bobber rig. Clip a 1/0 or 2/0 hook to the end of a wire leader. Add a couple of split shot above the leader and add a large round bobber at a depth that holds the minnow up off the bottom.

Cast this rig to weedlines, points or other structure. When the bobber goes under, give the fish slack as it makes its first run with the bait. When the pike stops, reel in slack line, feel for the fish and set the hook hard!

How to Fish Small Streams

Streams can be divided into two classifications: warm- and cold-water. Warm-water streams harbor typical warm-water species: bass, sunfish, catfish and white bass. They range in character from clear, fast-moving, whitewater-and-rock streams to muddy, slow, deep streams.

Cold-water streams are normally found at higher altitudes or in valleys that drain highlands. Their primary gamefish are various trout species. Cold-water streams are usually clean and fairly shallow, and they have a medium-to-fast current. Their bottoms are typically rock, gravel or sand. You can fish small streams by any of three methods: bank-fishing, wading or floating.

When wade-fishing, you should work upstream,

since you'll continually stir up silt and debris. By fishing upcurrent, sediment drifts behind you instead of in front of you, so the fish aren't alerted to your presence.

Floating takes more planning and effort than wading, but it may also offer greater rewards. On many streams, floating can take you into semi-virgin fishing territory. I prefer a canoe when float-fishing, but johnboats and inflatables also work.

Analyzing Small Streams

Current is the primary influence in the life of a stream. Current determines where fish will find food and cover and is why stream fishermen must always be aware how it affects fish location.

Fish react to current in one of three ways. They may be out in fast water chasing food; they might position themselves in an eddy at the edge of current where they can watch for food without using much energy; and they will locate in quiet pools where current is slow.

The typical stream is made up of a series of shallow riffles where current is swift, deep pools where current is slow and medium-depth runs where current is intermediate. Riffles normally empty into deep pools. Runs usually drain the downstream ends of pools, and these runs lead to successive riffles. In addition, rocks, logs, stumps and weeds form attractive stream cover. Many stream fish like to hide under or close to cover and dart out to grab a crawfish or minnow.

Analyzing a stream is a matter of studying the current, depth and cover. Remember that stream fish are consistent in the types of places where they hold. Catch one fish from behind a log, and chances are others will be hiding behind other logs.

Techniques for Fishing Small Streams

Stream fish are more confined than lake or reservoir fish. In big waters, fish have a lot of room to move around, but in streams, they have to be somewhere along one narrow waterway.

Bass – Smallmouth bass hold in eddies behind or under cover adjacent to fast current. Typical spots would be behind a rock or a root wad that splits the current, beneath an undercut bank that lies beside a fast run, along edges (and especially ends) of weedbeds, or under a lip or rocky bar at the head of a pool where a riffle empties into it. I always pay special attention to holes gouged out

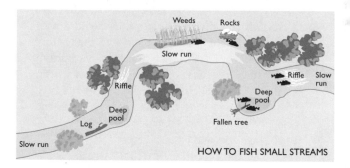

HOW TO FISH SMALL STREAMS

where a stream makes a turn.

Smallmouth bass prefer shade to bright sunshine. Any place that offers quiet water and concealment with access to fast water is a potential smallmouth hot spot. Depth of such locations can vary. To fish these places, I recommend spinning or spin-cast tackle and 4- to 8-pound test line. You'll need something fairly light, because most stream smallmouth baits are small.

These fish feed mostly on crawfish, minnows, worms, mature insects and insect larvae. The best artificial baits imitate these natural foods. Small crawfish crankbaits are deadly. So are floating minnows, in-line spinners, small jigs (hair or rubber skirt) and 4-inch plastic worms (like the Slider). But my favorite lure for stream smallmouth is a brown tube lure rigged on a small jighead.

The key with all these baits is to work them close to cover. Cast your lure across or up the current, and work it right through the spot where you think bass might be holding. I like to swim a tube lure parallel to a log or deep-cut bank. I also like to crawl a crawfish crankbait or float a minnow lure over logs, rocks or stumps. I'll cast a jig into the head of a pool, allow it to sink, then hop it across bottom back through the heart of the pool. At times, stream smallmouth will show a preference for one type of bait. In early spring, floating minnows or in-line spinners seem to work best. Later on, tube lures, small crankbaits and jigs are better.

One of the secrets of catching stream smallmouth on artificial lures is accurate casting. When stream-fishing, wear camouflage or natural colors that won't spook fish. Ease in from a downstream or cross-stream position of where the fish should be. Use the current and your rod tip to steer the bait into the strike zone.

Smallmouth can be taken on several live baits, but crawfish and spring lizards are best. Use a slip-sinker rig (#1 hook) to work through high-percentage spots. Ease baits slowly along bottom, and set the hook at the first hint of a pickup.

Many slower, deeper streams will hold large-mouth instead of smallmouth. Fish for largemouth just like you would for smallmouth.

Catfish – Channel and flathead catfish are common in warm-water streams. They usually stay in deep, quiet holes. When feeding, they move into current areas and watch for food washing by.

Fish pools, heads of pools or around cover in runs with moderate current. Use a bottom rig or a fixed-bobber rig and live bait. The weight of these rigs depends on the water depth and current.

Bait with worms, crawfish, fish guts, live minnows, cut bait or grasshoppers. Cast into the target zone, let the bait settle and wait for a bite. Early and late in the day (or at night), concentrate on the heads of pools. During mid-day, work the deeper pools and mid-depth runs. Be patient.

Trout – are found in cold-water streams throughout much of the United States and Canada. To catch these elusive fish, stay back from feeding zones, remain quiet, wear drab-colored clothes and cast beyond where you think the fish are located.

Trout prefer eddies adjacent to swift water where they can hide and dart out to grab passing food. During insect hatches, trout also feed in open runs with moderate current.

Since most trout streams are clear, rig with 4- to 6-pound test line. Then tie on a small in-line spinner, spoon, floating minnow or crawfish crankbait. Cast these lures around rocks, logs and other likely structure bordering swift water. The heads of pools can be especially good early in the morning and late in the afternoon.

Natural baits are effective on stream trout. Night crawlers, salmon eggs, grasshoppers and minnows are good bets. Canned corn or small marshmallows will tempt bites, especially from hatchery-raised trout. Also, various commercial "trout nibbles" are very effective. All these baits should be fished on the bottom with a very small hook (#12) and a split shot clamped 10-12 inches up the line.

How to Fish Large Rivers

Big rivers are just little streams that have grown up. They are more complex, however, and contain a much broader range of fishing conditions. They contain a wide variety of fishing locations: eddies, bluffs, dropoffs, shallow flats, feeder streams, backwater sloughs, tailwaters, deep and shallow areas, and swift-flowing and calm water.

As with small streams, large rivers are also divided into two types: warm and cold water. Most rivers in North America are the warm, deep variety, supporting sunfish, bass, catfish, walleye, etc.

In contrast, cold-water rivers are typically shallow and swift, flow through mountainous areas and usually hold various trout species.

Large rivers are most often fished from boats, though you can fish successfully from the bank, especially below dams or in backwaters and oxbows.

Analyzing Large Rivers

As in small streams, current determines fish locations in large rivers. Understanding current and being able to read rivers is essential to fishing them.

Current in large rivers may be more difficult to figure out. In small streams you can see the riffles and swift runs, but in large rivers the current may appear equal from bank to bank. Look closer, though, and you'll see signs of current breaks. Points of islands, jetties, dam tailwaters, river bars and mouths of tributaries are all areas where current is altered, and are prime spots to catch fish.

Most fish in large rivers hang in eddies or slack water. Sometimes they prefer still water bordering strong current where they can ambush baitfish. Besides current, three other variables in large rivers are water level, color and cover.

Water Level – Rivers continuously rise and fall, depending on the amount of rainfall upstream. The level of the river is referred to as its "stage" and this can have a direct bearing on fish locations.

Many times, when a river is rising and its waters are flooding surrounding lowlands, fish move into these freshly-flooded areas to take advantage of a banquet of worms, crawfish and other food.

Color – Large rivers vary greatly in water clarity. While the main channel area may be muddy, backwaters can be clear and more attractive to fish. Or, entire river systems may be muddy or clear, depending on recent rains. Most fish species feed better in clear rather than muddy water.

Cover – Fish react to cover in rivers the same way they do in other bodies of water. Bass, crappie and sunfish usually hold close to cover. Structure provides hiding places and a shield from current.

Techniques for Fishing Large Rivers

The key to catching fish in rivers is first in finding them and then applying the fundamentals of tackle, bait and fishing methods.

Sunfish – Sunfish tend to like quiet water, not current, so look for them in eddies, backwater sloughs, feeder creeks and other still areas. Remember that these fish won't linger in strong current very long, so find quiet, deep pools that have some structure.

Fish for them just like you would anywhere else. Use light tackle and small bobber rigs. Bait with worms, crickets or tiny tube jigs. Toss the bait right beside or into the cover, and wait for a bite.

Crappie – Crappie also prefer quiet water. The best places to find river crappie are sloughs and slow-moving tributaries. Sometimes crappie hold in brush and other cover along river banks where the current is slow to moderate in speed.

The best times to catch river crappie are spring and fall, and the easiest method is to move from one piece of cover to the next. Use a long panfish pole and a fixed-bobber rig to drop a minnow or small crappie jig around brush or vegetation. A good time for crappie is when a river is rising to flood adjacent sloughs and creeks. As the river rises, crappie move into cover in these areas.

Bass – In spring, look for river bass in quiet waters where current won't disturb their spawning beds. Cast to cover: brush, fallen trees, riprap banks, bridge pilings, etc. Spinnerbaits, buzzbaits, crankbaits, floating minnows and jigs are good lure choices.

By early summer, most river bass move out to the main channel where the biggest concentrations of baitfish are found. Bass in current breaks can dart out and nail minnows in the flow.

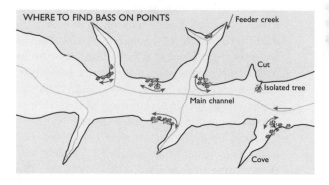

WHERE TO FIND BASS ON POINTS — Feeder creek — Cut — Isolated tree — Main channel — Cove

A variety of spots will hold river bass in summer and fall. These include mouths of feeder creeks, eddies on the sides and downstream ends of islands, rock piles, ends and sides of jetties that extend into the channel, riprap causeways, trees or logs washed up on a flat and wing walls in tailwaters. As in small streams, cast wherever the current is deflected by some object or feature in the river.

An increase in current can be a key to catching river bass. Many rivers have power dams and when the dams begin generating, the current increases suddenly. Bass that have been inactive will move to ambush stations and start feeding.

Lure choices for fishing rivers run the gamut. Minnow-imitating crankbaits (diving and lipless) and buzz baits are good in eddy pools, sand and mud bars, rock piles and rock jetties. Spinnerbaits are a top choice for working logs, treetops, brush and weeds. Jigs tipped with a pork or plastic trailer will snare bass from tight spots close to cover. Select lures for rivers as you would in lakes.

When a river floods adjacent lowlands, bass move into this fresh habitat to feed. Look for areas where the water is fairly clear and current is slack. Fish them with spinnerbaits, topwaters, shallow crankbaits or plastic worms. When the water starts dropping, bass will abandon these areas and move back to deeper water.

Always be conscious of river bass "patterns." If you find fish at the mouth of a feeder creek, chances are the next creek will also hold bass. The same is true of jetties, islands, rocks, etc.

Catfish and Bullheads – Both catfish and bullheads are plentiful in most large warm-water rivers. In the daytime, catfish stay in deep holes and channel edges, while bullheads prefer shallower backwaters. The best time to try for these fish is just after sundown. Fish for catfish along bluffs, tributary mouths, flats bordering the channel or the downstream side of rock jetties.

For catfish, use stout tackle and a bottom rig. Sinkers should be heavy enough to keep the bait anchored in current (1-3 oz.). Hooks should be large and stout (1/0-3/0 steel). Live minnows, worms or any traditional catfish bait will work. Cast the rig and allow it to sink to the bottom. Prop up the rod and wait for a bite.

A rock bank out of direct current will offer red-hot catfishing during spawning time. Fish these spots with a fixed or slip-bobber rig, adjusting the float so the bait hangs just above the rocks.

River catfishing can be phenomenal in dam tailwaters. Tailwaters contain baitfish, current, oxygenated water and bottom structure where fish can hold and feed. The best way to fish a tailwater is to work eddies close to the water that pours through the dam. If you're bank fishing, use a bottom rig and cast into quiet waters behind wing walls, pilings or the dam face. If the bottom is rough and you keep hanging up, switch to a slip-float rig adjusted so the bait hangs close to bottom.

A better way to fish tailwaters is from a boat,

floating along current breaks while bumping a two-hook panfish rig off the bottom. Use enough weight so your line hangs almost straight under the boat. Make long downstream drifts before motoring back for another float.

Just after a hard rain, look for gulleys and drains where fresh water rushes into the river. Catfish often move below these inflows and feed furiously. In this case, use a fixed or slip-bobber rig and dangle a bait only 2-3 feet under the surface in the immediate vicinity of the inflow.

Walleye – River walleye collect in fairly predictable places. They prefer to stay out of current, so look for them around islands, jetties, eddies below dams, etc. They usually hold near the edge of an eddy where they can watch for food.

The best river condition for catching walleye is when the water is low, stable and relatively clear. Walleye continue feeding when a river rises, but they may change locations. When the river gets too muddy, or when the water starts dropping, walleye generally become inactive.

Tailwaters below dams are among the best places to catch river walleye. Some fish stay in tailwaters all year long, but the biggest concentrations occur during winter and early spring. Walleye may hold close to dam faces or behind wingwalls. They also hang along rock ledges, gravel bars or other structure. But again, the key is reduced flow.

Boat-fishing is best for catching river walleye. Use a jig tipped with a live minnow, matching your jig weight to the amount of current. In slack water, a ⅛-oz. jig is heavy enough to work most tailwater areas. Float or troll through likely walleye spots, jigging vertically off the bottom. Or anchor and cast into eddies, holes and current breaks. Let the jig sink to the bottom, and work it back with a lift/drop retrieve. Always, work the bait slowly.

When bank fishing in early spring, cast crankbaits or jigs tipped with minnows along riprap banks. In summer and fall, look for walleye downstream, along riprap banks, jetties, gravel bars and creek mouths. Cast jigs or troll live-bait through deeper areas, or cast crankbaits along rocky shallows.

Northern Pike – Use the same tactics, tackle and baits for pike in large rivers that you would use in large lakes and reservoirs. The best places to look for river pike are in backwaters. They often hold in sloughs, marshes and tributaries away from the main channel. Cast to logs, brush or other shallow cover.

As in lakes and reservoirs, river pike are most active in spring, early summer and fall. A bonus time to fish for pike is whenever a river is rising and flooding adjacent lowlands.

8. WHEN FISH AREN'T BITING

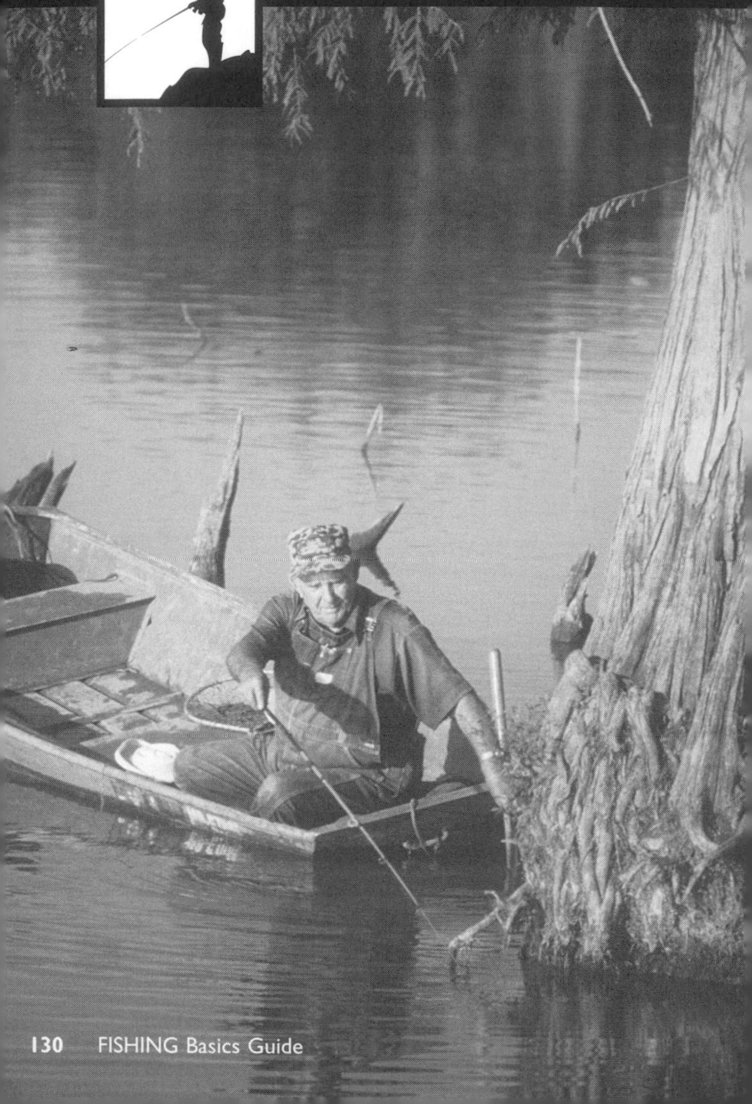

Every fisherman has days when the fish just won't bite! You try your best places, baits and techniques, but you can't get a nibble. It's as if the fish don't exist. So, what do you do? Give up and go home?

Hardly! On some days fish are just less active and more difficult to get to bite. But there are still tricks to try to get some action. Feeding patterns change from day to day, or even hour to hour. One thing is for sure, if you give up and go home, you're certain not to catch anything. But if you stay and keep experimenting with different baits and techniques, you've still got a chance of hitting on the right combination and making a good catch.

If fish aren't biting, don't give up. Instead, start changing all the variables you can like places, baits, methods and hopefully you'll hit the right combination.

Factors that Affect Fish Behavior

The fish's world is an ever-changing one. There's always something going on beneath the surface. Weather, water and food conditions are constantly shifting, and this has a strong effect on a fish's mood and activity level. Some sets of conditions cause fish to feed. Others turn them off.

This is why fishermen must be alert to condition changes and versatile in terms of adapting to them. They must analyze conditions when they get to their fishing spot and then make a logical decision about where fish are holding and the best bait and presentation to catch them. Following are factors that affect fish activity levels.

How Weather Affects Fish

Weather is one condition that affects every fishing trip. It may be hot or cold, sunny or cloudy, windy or calm or dry or rainy. It may be a period of stable weather, or a time of changing weather. Sometimes weather will help (cause fish to bite), and sometimes it will hurt (cause fish to quit biting).

Fish are sensitive to weather changes, such as a sudden shower, a passing cold front, rising or falling barometer, etc. Here is how they react.

Air Temperature – Water temperature is mainly regulated by air temperature. The warmer the air temperature, the warmer the water. Fish are cold-blooded, so their metabolism is controlled by water temperature. In warmer water, fish use up their food faster and feed more often. On the other hand, in cool or cold water, a fish's metabolism slows down, and they don't have to feed as often. This is why fish are usually more active in warm water than in cooler water. (One exception is when very warm water is cooled by rain or a quick drop in air temperature. In very warm water, fish sometimes slip into a semi-active state, but a sudden temperature drop can trigger a feeding spree.)

Sky Condition – Sky condition plays a big part in where fish are located. On cloudy days fish are more likely to be in shallow water and roaming around weeds, brush, docks, etc. But when bright sunshine penetrates the water (especially during mid-day), fish will usually retreat back into deeper water or shady areas. Rarely do fish stay in shallow, open water during bright sunny conditions.

Precipitation – It's an old saying that fish bite better when it's raining. There is some truth in this if the rain is light. A light to moderate rain creates positives: cloudy sky, surface disturbance, runoff washing nutrients into the water, new color from mud, sudden cooling of water and a fresh infusion of oxygen into the water. All can stimulate feeding.

Wind – Wind makes fish more likely to bite. Wind driven currents push baitfish into predictable feeding areas. Waves stir up mud along shorelines, adding color and dislodging nutrients. Waves break up the surface and add oxygen to the water. Like rain, these things all cause fish to feed. This is why it's usually better to fish the wind-exposed side of a lake rather than the sheltered side.

Barometric Pressure – Fish have a keen ability to sense changes in barometric pressure, and they respond by becoming more or less active. Fish are usually more active when the barometer is dropping, or when it's been high and steady for a couple of days. Fish are typically less active right after a sudden rise in barometric pressure.

One of the best times to go fishing is right before a storm or cold front passes. In these situations, the barometer may drop rapidly. Fish sense the rapid drop in pressure and sometimes go on a feeding binge. After the front passes, the fish usually quit feeding.

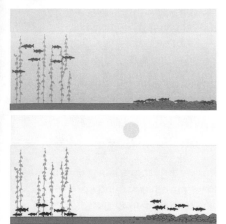

Light plays a key role in fish location. In overcast conditions (above) fish are likely to move into shallow water and move around in weeds and brush. Occasionally they will remain inactive near the bottom. In bright, sunny conditions, (bottom) light penetrates the water and fish will usually retreat into deeper water or shade.

Water Conditions and Fish

Water conditions are frequently tied to weather. These include water temperature, clarity, water level, amount of dissolved oxygen and currents.

Water Temperature – Fish seek areas where water temperature is most comfortable to them. This comfort zone varies from species to species. Warm water species (bass, sunfish, catfish) prefer a range of 70-85°F. Cool water species (walleye, pike, muskies) like a range of 60-70°F. Cold water species (trout, salmon) prefer 50-60°F.

These ranges are preferences. Depending on time of year and prevailing water temperatures, fish are often found in water that's outside their preferred zone. However, they're usually more active when they're in their preferred range.

In many lakes and reservoirs, water temperature will change from the surface down to the depths. Water temperature near the surface changes faster than deeper water. Surface water warms faster in the day and cools off faster at night.

So, how does this help you find and catch fish? Say you're a bass fisherman on a lake in the middle of summer. The local fishing report gives the surface temperature at 80°F. You would expect most fish to be in deep water or in heavy, shady cover, since these areas would be cooler and more to their liking. But at night, as the surface temperature cools off, bass might move up to shallow water where they'd be more accessible to anglers.

On the other hand, in early spring, water surface temperature might be 55°F at dawn, but on a sunny day it might warm into the 60°F range by mid-day. In this case, the bass would be more active during this warmer period. Then their activity level would drop off as the water cools at dusk.

Many expert anglers use thermometers to check water temperature. Be aware that water temperature plays an important role in where fish are and how active they'll be.

Water Clarity – When anglers talk about water color, they mean water clarity. Some lakes, reservoirs and streams are clear with good underwater visibility, others are dingy, and still others are muddy. Water clarity changes frequently when it rains (mud is washed into the lake) or when strong winds stir up mud along the shore.

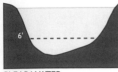

CLEAR WATER
Lure disappears at 6 feet plus

STAINED WATER
Lure disappears at 2-6 feet

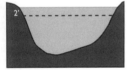

DARK WATER
Lure disappears at 0-2 feet

In clear water, fish usually hold deeper or tighter to brush, docks, rocks, etc. than fish in dingy or muddy water. This is because when visibility is better, fish are more vulnerable to predators. In muddy water, they're hidden by the water color and stay shallower, and feel safer away from cover.

As a rule of thumb, the best water to fish is slightly to moderately dingy. The fish will be shallower and not so spooky, yet there's enough visibility for them to see to feed. Extremely muddy water hampers a fish's ability to find food (and baits)! Only scent-feeding species like catfish are active in really muddy water.

Water Level – Water levels in lakes, reservoirs and rivers may rise or fall, depending on rain, water discharges from dams, or seasonal fluctuations. As a general rule, fish follow a rise (i.e., go shallow when the water is rising), then they move out deeper when the water level is falling.

In lakes and reservoirs, rising water makes fresh food available. Also, in rivers and streams, rising water washes new food downstream.

Falling water levels have the opposite effect. Fish pull back into deeper areas. If the water drop is gradual, they may continue to feed normally. But if the drop is fast, they may quit feeding.

Current – A good way to think of current is liquid wind. Current pushes food in the direction it's moving. Predator fish know this, and rely on current to carry food to them.

Currents in rivers and streams are continuous, though they may increase or decrease depending on water flow. Also prevailing winds will push water onto shore or through narrow areas between points or islands and fish move into these areas to feed. This is why fishing on the downwind shoreline is often better than on the upwind shoreline. Many times, fishing in windy areas is better than in calm areas.

HOW THE MOON AFFECTS FISHING

Many media fishing forecasts list "best feeding times" or "solunar periods." These are calculated according to when the moon exerts tidal pull.

Here's the theory. The moon's pull causes tides in the oceans, and saltwater anglers know that when the tide is running, the fishing is better. The same thing happens on freshwater lakes and reservoirs, but on a much smaller scale.

Many experts believe that these gravity changes influence feeding behavior. The charts usually list two "major feeding periods" and two "minor feeding periods" each day.

I believe these moon times may have some merit, but may be secondary to other factors in determining whether fish will bite. I think fish feed better during major and minor periods than they do between these periods.

Fishing records also show that during the four-day period around the full moon, big fish are definitely more active. The days of the month between the full and new moons are the least productive.

9. PLAY, LAND AND HANDLE FISH

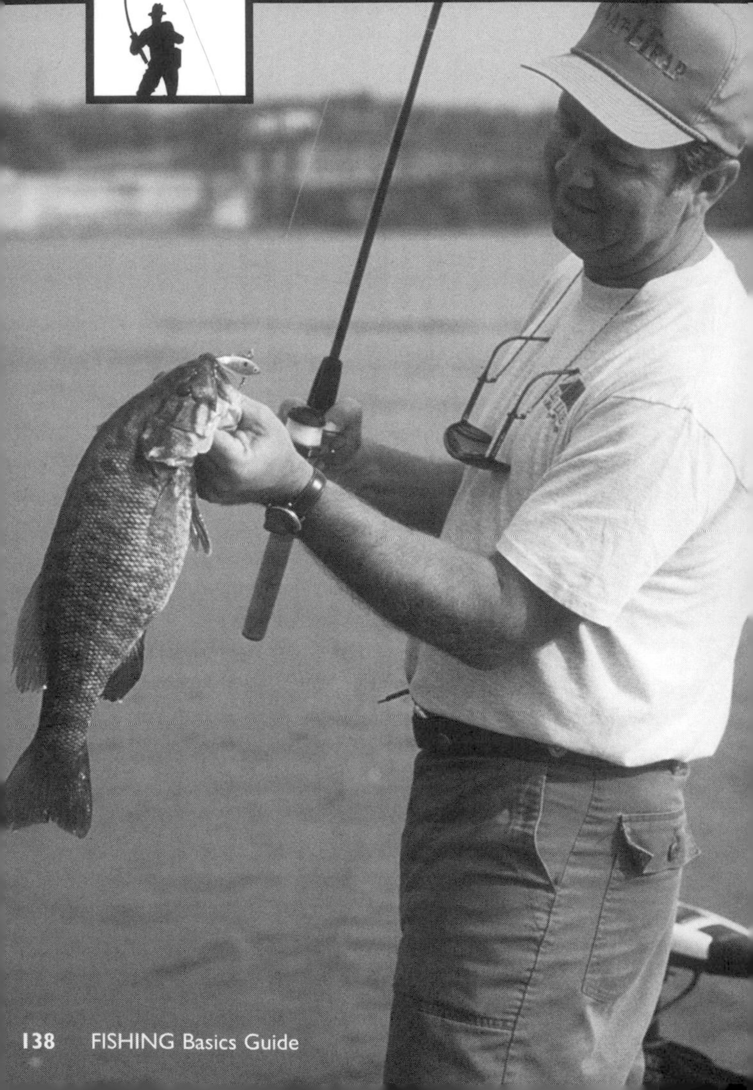

One of the great thrills in fishing is hooking and playing a big fish, and one of the heartbreaks is losing it! All fishermen want to catch a big one. It's an integral part of the sport. And all fishermen taste disappointment when a lunker comes off, even when they would have released it alive if they'd landed it. Still, it's the uncertainty of this sport that makes it exciting. If you knew you'd land every fish you hooked, fishing wouldn't be nearly as much fun.

This isn't to say that you shouldn't try to land every fish you hook. You should, and this is why you need to learn proper playing, landing and handling methods. By using the right techniques, you'll enjoy the "thrill of victory" more often. In the following pages, you'll learn to play a fish to keep the odds in your favor; how to land fish from a boat or on shore; and how to handle fish both for your safety and for their well being in case you want to release them alive and well.

Fine Art of "Playing" Fish

Playing fish and fighting fish mean the same thing. These are terms for tiring a fish out and reeling it close enough to capture. Playing small fish is easy; they don't have as much size or fight, but playing a big fish can be a tough head-to-head battle.

There are two overall "concepts" for playing fish. One is to play them with the main purpose of having fun, of stretching the fight out and giving the fish maximum opportunity to get away. Anglers who like to do this frequently use light or ultra light tackle because it takes more finesse to land fish with light tackle. With this tackle, you don't have as much control over the fish. You can't power them in, so you have to wear them down more. The longer a fight lasts, the greater the odds of the fish getting away.

The second way to play fish is with the purpose of landing them as fast and efficiently as possible. They are more concerned with the end result – landing fish – than how they land them. Tournament anglers or those fishing for food are more likely to use these "power" methods, which typically involve heavier tackle and stronger line.

Each angler must decide which approach he prefers. Neither is more or less acceptable than the other. They are just different playing styles for different purposes and philosophies.

Pointers for "Playing" Fish

These are pointers for playing large bass, walleye, stripers, pike, catfish, muskies and other big fish.

Rule number one is to keep the line tight at all times. This is no problem if the fish is pulling against you. But if it's running toward you, reel in line fast enough to keep out slack. When a fish jumps, it's easier for it to throw a lure or hook if the line is slack. Therefore, when a fish goes airborne, keep the line tight to control headshakes. Many experts try to prevent or control jumps by keeping the rod tip low or even poking it in the water when a fish starts up. Sometimes this downward pressure will cause the fish to turn back down.

When fighting a fish, use the bend of the rod to tire it out. Except during jumps (when you're pointing the rod down), hold the rod or pole high with maximum bend.

You must adjust your playing technique to the type of tackle you're using. Obviously, if you're using light tackle, you can't exert as much pressure on a fish as you can with heavier tackle. On the other hand, if you're fishing around thick cover (brush, weeds, timber, docks, etc.), you may have to apply maximum pressure to keep a fish from burrowing in and tangling your line. Use heavier tackle and line when fishing thick cover. This will allow you to apply more pressure to turn a fish.

With really big fish, a pump-and-reel technique works well. Lift the rod slowly and steadily to pull the fish toward the surface. Then reel in the line as you lower your rod tip back down. Repeat this process, always keep the line tight. This keeps constant pressure on a fish and tires it quickly.

Don't be in too much of a hurry. If you "overplay" a fish by reeling in too fast, you risk pulling the hook out or breaking your line. Unless a fish is headed for thick cover, keep steady pressure and let the fish tire out before you try to land it.

How to Set and Use Drag

Drag is an elemental concept in playing fish, and it's one that all rod-and-reel anglers must learn to use. Basically, drag is a slip-clutch mechanism built into a reel that allows line to slip out when a pre-set amount of pressure is exerted on the line. It is a safeguard against pulling so hard against a fighting fish that you break your line. Drag settings are adjustable, and drag should be set at some point below the break strength of your line. Then, when a fish applies this amount of pull, the drag will slip and give line rather than allowing pressure to build to the breaking point.

For example, say you're using 8-pound test line. You might set your drag to slip at 6 pounds of pressure. Then, if you hook a big fish and it makes a strong run, the drag will give before the line snaps. As the fish tires and stops pulling drag, you can reel in line and land the fish.

When a fish is pulling out drag, don't keep turning the reel handle, this can cause line twist in the reel. Instead, hold the reel handle steady until the fish stops running or until it turns back toward you. Then begin reeling again to keep tension on the line as you play the fish.

Two Methods for Setting Drag

Setting the proper amount of drag can be a complicated process. Several factors go into knowing how much drag is just right. Strength of the line, weight and strength of the fish, how much line is out, and the amount of line on the reel spool all affect how much drag is needed. Also, conditions that determine the optimum drag setting can change rapidly when fighting a fish.

Obviously, you won't know these variables before you start fishing, so drag must be pre-set according to the "best guess" method. Many fishing experts set drag to give at half the rated break strength of the line. For instance, for 6-pound test line, set the drag to slip at 3 pounds of pressure.

This method for setting drag is precise, but it takes more effort. Tie one end of a small fish-weighing scale to a stationary object. Then tie your fishing line to the other end. Disengage the reel spool or trip the bail and back away approximately 20 yards. Then re-engage the spool or bail. Hold the rod at a 90-degree angle to the scale (just like you're fighting a fish), and reel the line tight. Then start pulling the line with the rod while adjusting the drag setting. Have a friend watch the scale and tell you when you're pulling out the desired amount of pressure. Adjust the drag so it slips at this weight. Then it's properly set.

Another method for setting drag is the "feels-right" method. You simply run the line through the rod guides. Then hold the rod handle with one hand and pull the line off the reel with the other. Adjust the drag setting to slip before the line snaps. This method isn't nearly as accurate as using the scale, but it's much faster.

Also, remember that you can readjust drag setting whenever you wish while actually fighting a fish. Baitcasting and spin-cast reels have star drags next to the reel handle that can be tightened or loosened as desired. Spinning reels have knobs either on the front of the spool or behind the gearbox that can be turned to tighten or loosen drag as desired.

Overall, knowing how to use drag properly is a mark of an accomplished fisherman. Proper use of drag will allow you to catch many more fish in the course of your angling career.

How to Land Fish

Landing a fish is the end-result of playing it. This is the actual capture, when you net, grab or beach a fish. Regardless of where or how you're fishing, the number one rule in landing is to make sure the fish is tired out. Too many anglers try to land fish while they are "green" (still have some fight left), and the fish escapes in a last-ditch lunge. So, unless you plan to release the fish alive, play it down to the point where it's easier to handle.

If you're fishing from a bank that slopes gently into the water, simply drag the fish onto land. If the bank is steep, or if you're fishing from a boat, lift the fish out of the water with your rod or pole. To do this, however, use line that has a higher pound-test rating than the weight of the fish. If you try to lift a 6-pound bass with 4-pound line, the line will break.

When beaching or lifting a fish, it helps to have the fish's momentum going in the direction you're trying to move it. If the fish is swimming, you can steer it up on the bank or into shallow water where you can grab it.

Nets are great for landing fish from the bank, from a boat or when wading. The netting procedure is always the same. After the fish is played down and under control, lift its head out of the water with gentle rod pressure. Then lead the fish headfirst into a stationary net held just below the water's surface. When the fish is in or over the net, lift up. Never chase or stab at a fish with a landing net, and never attempt to net a fish tail-first.

A third common way to land fish is by hand. In doing so, you must be extremely careful. Sharp fins, teeth and spines can inflict painful injuries.

There are two ways to land fish by hand. Species that don't have teeth can be grabbed and lifted by the lower jaw. Reel the fish up close and lift its head out of the water with rod pressure. Then stick your thumb in the fish's mouth, clamp the lower jaw between your thumb and forefinger and lift the fish from the water.

Species that have teeth, however, should be grabbed across the back, pinching firmly on both gill plates. They may also be lifted by placing a hand under the belly. In either case, the fish must be played down fully before you land it.

Many anglers also land fish by inserting their fingers into the gills or by squeezing thumb and forefinger into the fish's eye sockets. These methods work, but are not recommended. Some species have sharp gill plates that can inflict a nasty cut. Also, if a fish is to be released alive, its gills or eyes can be damaged by such rough treatment.

10. BOATS, MOTORS AND ACCESSORIES

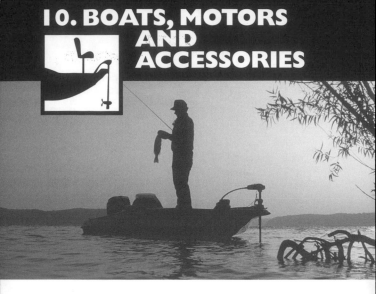

Most beginners will start fishing from the bank, bridge or dock. But sooner or later, as your skills increase, you'll want to broaden your horizons and get out on the water.

It's not that you can't catch fish around the banks. You certainly can, but having a boat allows you to step up to another level in fishing. It opens a whole new world, permitting you to cover more water and be more versatile in your approach to the sport. A boat expands your fishing opportunities, and allows you to increase your knowledge and fun.

Types of Boats

Fishing boats come in a broad range of designs and prices. High end bass boats cost in the mid-$40,000 range! On the low end are float tubes that start around $50. The expensive rigs are highly technical and ultimately functional, but we'll stick to the basic, less expensive, easier-to-maintain models that beginning anglers are more likely to buy. These include johnboats, V-hulls, canoes, bass buggies and float tubes.

Following are looks at each of these types of boats, the waters where they work best and their advantages and disadvantages.

Johnboats – The aluminum johnboat may be the best all-purpose fishing boat for beginners. Johnboats have a flat bottom and a square or semi-V-bow design. They are very stable and draw only a few inches of water, which enables them to traverse shallow areas. Johnboats were designed for streams, but a deep-sided, wide-beamed johnboat also adapts well to large open lakes. These boats perform well with outboard motors.

Johnboats come in a range of lengths, from 8 to more than 20 feet. But the 12- and 14-foot models are most popular. These are light enough to be cartopped and carried to the water by two anglers. This means you can use a johnboat wherever you can drive close to a stream, pond or lakeshore.

Johnboats have three minor disadvantages: the flat hull provides a rough ride in choppy water; johnboats are clumsy to paddle; because of their all-metal construction, they are noisy when objects are dropped or banged against the sides.

V-hull – These are the workhorses of fishing boats. It's called V-hull because it has a V-shaped bow that tapers back to a flat-bottomed hull. This allows the V-hull to slice through waves, giving a smoother, safer ride in rough water.

Most are made of fiberglass or aluminum. Heavier fiberglass boats provide a smoother ride in choppy water. Most popular V-hull sizes are 12 to18 feet and are normally fitted with mid-sized outboards (25-100 horsepower).

A disadvantage of the V-hull is it's weight. Larger V-hulls require trailers, and must be launched from ramps. They are awkward to paddle, but maneuver well with an electric trolling motor.

These boats are the standard on big lakes and rivers because of their ability to handle rough water. As with johnboats, they are often customized with a broad range of accessories. Some models are equipped with console steering. V-hull boats range from basic no-frills boats to those with a motor and numerous factory-installed accessories.

Canoes – They suffer from bad PR. Inexperienced canoeists believe these boats are too tippy for fishing. The truth is, certain models are very stable, and make excellent fishing boats for a wide range of waters.

Canoes offer anglers several advantages. They are relatively inexpensive and are extremely portable. They can be car-topped and carried to lakes or streams far off the beaten path. They are also ideal for small waters where bigger boats are impractical or even disallowed. Canoes draw only inches of water, are highly maneuverable and can be paddled through shallow riffles or bays.

Canoes are made from several materials: fiberglass, aluminum and polyethylene. They come in square stern and double-end models. (Square stern canoes are best for using outboards or electric motors. Motors may also be used on double-end canoes with a side-mount bracket near the stern.) A 16- or 17-foot canoe has a wide beam and flat bottom offering the greatest stability and versatility.

Float Tube – Float tubes, also called belly boats, are not true boats like the others mentioned in this chapter. A float tube is a floating doughnut with a sewn-in seat and leg holes. An angler carries it to his fishing site, steps in, pulls it up around his waist, then walks into the water. When he's deep enough for the float tube to support his weight, he propels himself by kicking with swim fins or special paddles attached to his boots.

Float tubes are used to fish close to shore in small, quiet waters. They're very maneuverable, but are slow. They're good for fishing in flooded brush, timber, patches of cattails or other spots that are difficult to reach by boat. Since float tubes are very quiet, they're good for slipping up on spooky fish.

Float tubes should not be used in strong-wind/open-lake situations. High waves can flip you upside down, and float tubes can be difficult to right.

Types of Motors

Motors aren't absolutely necessary for fishing, but in many cases they certainly make the job easier. You must decide if you need a motor by the type of boat you have and the water where you plan to fish. If you'll be using a small boat on remote streams, small ponds or lakes, paddles may be all the power you need. But if you'll be on larger waters where you'll have to cover more distance, or where winds or currents can be strong, a larger boat with a motor will be more practical and efficient.

Fishing motors come in two varieties: outboard and electric. Outboard (gas-powered) motors are more powerful and are used mainly for running long distances – getting from one spot to the next. Electric (battery-powered) motors are less powerful and much quieter. Their job is to ease the boat through the target area while the angler fishes. Electric motors are also used as the main power source on waters where outboards aren't allowed.

Outboard Motors – Often new outboard motors cost more than the boat they power. But

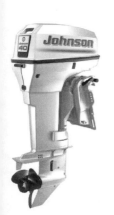

anglers should view them as a long-term investment. Outboards are dependable and easy to operate and will last many years if properly maintained. They range from 1.5 to 250-plus horsepower. Smaller motors are lightweight and portable and attach to the boat's stern with clamp mounts. Larger motors are heavy, and permanently bolted onto the stern.

The main consideration when buying a motor is not to overpower the boat. All boats list maximum horsepower ratings either on the stern plate or in the owner's instructions. Never exceed these ratings.

Electric Motors – Electrics fall into one of two categories: 12-volt and 24-volt. Twelve-volt motors are powered by one 12-volt battery. Twenty-four volt motors require two linked 12-volt batteries. The obvious difference between the two is available power, which is measured in "pounds of thrust." The 24-volt motor is much stronger than a 12-volt. Twenty-four volt motors are normally used on big boats that operate in rough water. On smaller boats and quiet waters, a 12-volt motor is adequate.

Electric motors have different types of mounts and methods of operation. Some have clamp-on mounts to fit on the sides or transom of the boat. Others have bow mounts that attach permanently to the bow. It is much more efficient for an electric motor to pull a boat rather than push it. A boat with an electric motor mounted on or near the bow is easier to propel and steer.

Some electrics are operated by hand, while others have foot controls that allow the user to run the motor while keeping his hands free to fish.

When shopping for an electric motor, you'll find models with many options and power ratings. My recommendation for a beginner's first electric

A fish finder's signal is interpreted as a grapic image on the LCD screen. The computer uses the transponder's signal to paint a picture of the bottom, features and hanging fish.

is a 12-volt clamp-on model with 20-40 pounds of thrust. Remember that the heavier your boat, the more power you'll need to pull or push it. Also, electric motor shafts come in different lengths. Owners of johnboats, canoes and bass buggies will probably need motors with shafts that are 30 or 36 inches long. Owners of V-hulls may need a motor with a 42-inch shaft, since these boats have higher sides and are more likely to be used in rolling waves.

Fish Locaters

A fish locater is an angler's eyes under the water. Its basic function is to show the bottom and objects between the surface and the bottom. Knowing water depth is important both from a safety standpoint and also for fishing efficiency. Fish locaters can show submerged structure: drop-offs, sunken channels, stumps, brush, rocks, weeds, etc. A good fish locater can even tell whether the bottom is soft or hard, and can pinpoint concentrations of bait- and gamefish.

Even though a fish finder is fairly expensive, it is considered an almost indispensable tool by serious anglers. I recommend one for anyone who will be fishing away from shore on lakes and large rivers. A fish locater, properly used will pay great dividends in terms of numbers of fish caught.

A fish locater is a sonar unit that emits sound waves. These strike underwater objects and the locater measures how long it takes the echoes to bounce back to the sending unit. The deeper an object, the longer the time required. The fish locater then translates this time into a distance display, showing bottom depth and suspended objects.

Most fish locaters are liquid crystal display (LCD) units that draw chart-like pictures of what's beneath the boat. The latest technology includes different colors in this display to help users distinguish between fish and other underwater features. You can actually see fish you're trying to catch!

Boat Accessories

The boat, motor and fish locater make up the core of the fishing rig, but several other accessories are needed to complete the package. State and federal laws require certain safety equipment on all boats. Boats under 16 feet must carry a Coast Guard-approved flotation device for each passenger, a paddle, some type of sound signal (whistle, air horn, etc.), running lights if the boat is to be used at night and a fire extinguisher if gas is kept in an enclosed compartment. Boats 16 feet and longer must meet these requirements, plus the flotation devices must be wearable life preservers and the boat must have a throwable flotation device (cushion, safety ring, etc). Contact your state water safety office for these requirements.

11. KEEPING AND CLEANING FISH

One of the real pleasures in life is a shore lunch – beaching your boat and cooking and eating fish that you've just caught. Fresh fillets cooked over an open fire are truly delicious. A morning of fishing guarantees a hearty appetite, and the fish will never be fresher or taste better. Throw in a skillet of home-fried potatoes, cole slaw and some hushpuppies, and you have a meal that rivals any served in the finest restaurants!

For many anglers, eating fish is the final reward in fishing. Fish are delicious, healthful and there's a special satisfaction in sharing your catch with friends and family. For fish to taste their best, however, they must be cleaned and kept properly. This process starts the moment the fish is landed.

Caring for Your Catch

When you keep fish to eat, be sure they stay fresh. This guarantees they will retain their best flavor for cooking. If fish aren't kept fresh, the flesh becomes mushy and strong-tasting.

There are two ways to ensure freshness: keep fish alive or keep them cold. Fish may be kept alive in a fish basket, on a stringer or in the live well of a boat if the water is cool and well-oxygenated. Or, fish can be killed and placed on ice as soon as they're caught.

When you fish from the bank, a simple rope or chain stringer is the easiest way to keep your catch. Punch the point of the stringer up through the fish's mouth; then pull the stringer through the open mouth. Do not string fish through the gills. This makes it hard for them to breathe and could cause them to die. In hot weather, it's best to put your fish on ice.

Dead fish that aren't placed on ice will spoil quickly. Check the eyes and gill color to determine freshness. If the eyes look clear and the gills are dark red, the fish are fresh. If the eyes are cloudy and the gills have turned pinkish-white, the fish are beginning to spoil.

Before putting fish in a cooler, give them a sharp rap with a blunt object (pliers, knife handle, etc.) on the spine just behind the eyes. This kills them quickly, which keeps them from flopping around in the cooler. Then place the fish on top of crushed ice in the cooler. Keep excess water drained away as the ice melts. Fish flesh gets mushy when soaked for an extended time.

Many anglers prefer to field-dress their fish before placing them on ice. This is done by cutting the gills and guts away with a small knife. These are the organs that spoil first, so this additional step helps ensure freshness.

Tools for Cleaning Fish

Any fish-cleaning method requires a sharp knife. I recommend a fillet knife. These knives have thin, sharp, flexible blades for easy cleaning. A knife with a 7-inch blade is adequate for cleaning most fish.

One good alternative to a fillet knife is an electric knife. Of course, fish cleaners must be careful not to cut themselves, and this is an even greater concern with an electric knife.

An inexpensive metal scaler with pointed teeth makes scaling fish much easier, but scaling can also be done with a metal spoon or a kitchen knife with a rigid blade. A fish-cleaning glove is optional; it protects your hand from nicks. A piece of ½-inch plywood makes a good cleaning platform, and you'll need two pans or buckets: one for the cleaned fish, and the other for remains.

Simple Methods for Cleaning Fish

Fish should be cleaned as soon after they're caught as possible. Don't leave fish in a cooler overnight. Clean and refrigerate them immediately. They will taste better, and you'll be glad you don't have to

STORING FISH FOR COOKING

Fish can be kept in the refrigerator for 2-3 days without losing much freshness. However, if longer storage is desired, they should be frozen.

To keep cleaned fish (whole, fillets or steaks) in the refrigerator, blot them dry with a paper towel. Then place them on a plate covered with paper towels and wrap them tightly with plastic wrap.

To freeze whole fish, place them inside a plastic milk jug (cut the top away) or large frozen food container, then cover them with water. Tap the sides of the container to release trapped air. Use masking tape to label the container with the type of fish and date they were caught. Then freeze.

To freeze fillets or steaks, place fish pieces in a double-walled Ziploc freezer bag (one bag inside another). Zip the inner bag almost closed, and suck all air out of this bag to form a vacuum. Then zip the inner bag closed. Do the same with the outer bag. The double thickness protects against freezer burn. Before freezing, label the outer bag with the type fish and date they were caught.

Fish frozen in either manner described above will keep 6 months or longer without losing their fresh flavor.

To thaw whole fish frozen in ice, run tap water over the container until the block of ice can be removed. Place this frozen block in a colander so melting water can drain. Thaw fish at room temperature. To thaw bagged fillets, place in a baking pan and thaw at room temperature. Cook fish as soon as possible after they're thawed.

face this cleaning chore the next day.

There are a number of options for cleaning fish. They can be scaled or skinned with the bones left intact, or they can be filleted (meat cut away from the bones). It's up to each angler's preference. Usually small fish (bluegill, perch) are scaled and cooked whole, but even they can be filleted. When fish are filleted by a skilled cleaner, little useable meat is wasted.

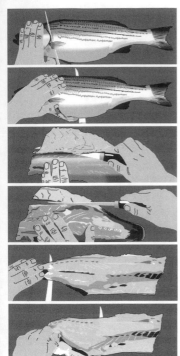

To fillet (1) Cut behind the pectoral fin to the backbone. (2) Separate the fillet, cutting along the backbone toward the tail. (3) Cut off the rib section by sliding the blade along the bones. (4) Cut off the belly fat. (5) With the skin side down, begin to cut from the tail. (6) Cut the skin from the fillet with a sawing motion.

Scaling – Scaling is the process of scraping the scales off the fish and then removing the heads and guts. The skin is left on and the bones remain intact. Small sunfish, crappie, walleye, bass and other species can all be scaled and cooked whole.

To scale a fish, lay it on its side. Hold the head with one hand, and scrape from the tail toward the head (against the grain). This will cause the scales to flake off. The sides are easy to scale with hard spots along the back, stomach and near the fins.

After scaling, cut the head off just behind the gills. Then slice the belly open and remove the guts. The tail and major fins may be cut off if desired. Finally, wash the fish thoroughly to remove loose

Skinning catfish. (1) Grip the head and slit the skin on both sides just behind the pectoral spines. (2) Slice the skin along the backbone to just behind the dorsal fin. (3) Use pliers to peel the skin off over the tail. (4) Pull the head down breaking the backbone and pull out the guts. (5) Remove the fins with pliers and slice off the tail.

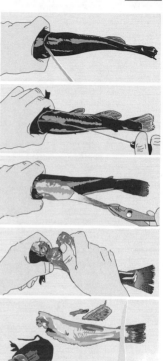

scales and blood.

Filleting – Many anglers prefer to fillet their fish for meat with no bones. Filleted fish are easy to cook and a pleasure to eat. Also, when filleting is mastered, it's faster than scaling. Experts can fillet a fish in less than a minute. The only drawback is losing a small amount of meat in the filleting process.

Skinning – Catfish and bullheads are covered by a slick skin instead of scales. These fish may be filleted as explained above, but many anglers prefer to skin and gut them. Catfish and bullheads may then be cooked whole, or bigger fish may be cut into steaks.

APPENDIX

Must-Have Fishing Accessories

Tackle Box/Bag – Every fisherman must have a tackle box or bag for toting tackle and gear. In essence, this is like a portable locker.

Fisherman's Tool – This is a fancy name for needle-nose pliers.

Line Clippers – This is an angler's term for fingernail clippers that are used for cutting line.

Fishing Cap – Fishermen need a good cap to block the sun off their face and shade their eyes.

Polarized Sunglasses – Sunglasses cut down on glare off the water, and polarized sunglasses actually allow you to see beneath the surface.

Fisherman's Towel – This is a convenience item, but it's very nice to have when handling fish or messy live bait.

Sunscreen – Having and using sunscreen is absolutely essential.

Fish Stringer – If you fish from the bank or from a boat that doesn't have a live well, you will need a fish stringer to keep your catch.

PFD (Personal Flotation Device) – A Coast Guard-certified PFD is required by law when fishing from a boat. (Always wear your life preserver when the boat is running.)

Rainsuit – A rainsuit is good for keeping you dry in a rainstorm.

Fishing Vest/Tackle Belt – A vest or tackle belt is extremely handy for fishing streams or ponds where you will walk a lot.

Tote Bag – A tote or duffle bag is handy for carrying fishing accessories that won't fit into a tackle box.

Live Bait Container – If you fish with live bait, you'll need a minnow bucket, worm box, cricket cage or some other container to keep your bait alive and healthy.

Camera – If you practice catch-and-release, a camera is handy for photographing trophy fish before you let them go. A digital camera is best, since you can download images and email them to friends.

Reel Repair Kit – A small reel repair kit can be a lifesaver for in-the-field repairs or adjustments. I carry a kit that includes small screwdrivers (flathead and Phillips), an adjustable wrench and a container of reel oil.

Lure Retriever – If you fish from a boat, a lure retriever can save a lot of money in lost lures. If you hang your lure on an underwater object, you can position the boat directly over the lure and use a retriever to free it. Lure retrievers come in two types: a heavy weight on a string, and a collapsible pole. The pole works better, but it's bulkier and more costly. A weight/string can be kept in a tackle box or tote bag.